A Brie
Islām and its l
Al-Qaec

Prophet Muḥammad (peace be upon him) said: "There will appear at the end of time a people who are young of age, foolish-minded. They will speak with the best (and most-alluring) of speech (that is spoken) by people and will recite the Qur'ān but it will not go beyond their throats. They will pass out of Islām as the arrow passes through its target. Whoever meets them, let him kill them, for there is a reward for whoever kills them." The Prophet's Companion,

Abū Umāmah al-Bāhilī (d. 700) said of the Khārijites (extremist renegades): "The Dogs of the people of Hellfire, they used to be Muslims but turned disbelievers." When Abū Umāmah was asked whether this was his own speech or something he heard from the Prophet, he said, "Rather, I heard it from the Prophet." The Salafī scholar and jurist,

Abu Bakr al-Ājurrī (d. 970) said: "The scholars have not differed that the Khārijite (extremists) are an evil people, disobedient to God and His Messenger, even if they pray, fast and strive hard in worship. None of that will be beneficial to them. They proclaim the commanding of good and prohibiting of evil but that will not benefit them because they distort the Qur'ān upon their desires and deceive the Muslims. God, the Most High, warned us against them. The Prophet warned us against them. The rightly-guided caliphs warned us against them. The Prophet's companions warned us against them. They are an evil, filthy despicable people." The famous Salafī scholar,

Ibn Taymiyyah (d. 1328) said: "For they – the Khārijite extremists – strived to kill every Muslim who did not agree with their view, declaring the blood of the Muslims, their wealth, and the slaying of their children to be lawful, while excommunicating them. And they considered this to be worship, due to their ignorance and their innovation which caused [them] to stray." The late Salafī scholar, **'Abd al-'Azīz bin Bāz** (d. 1999) said: "The correct view is that the Khārijite [extremists] are disbelievers." And finally, the late Salafī scholar, **Muḥammad bin Ṣāliḥ al-'Uthaymīn** (d. 2001) said: "If you were to look into the hearts [of the Khārijite terrorist extremists], you would find them black and hard. They accuse sinful Muslims of disbelief, but they are greater in disbelief."

This is the well-known, unequivocal, uncompromising Islāmic stance towards the extremist, terrorist renegades.

Title: A Brief Guide to Islām and its Position Towards al-Qaeda and ISIS
Author: Abū ʿIyāḍ Amjad bin Muḥammad Rafīq
Version: 4.50

2nd Edition, Rajab 1438 AH / April 2017 CE.
1st Edition, Rabīʿ al-Awwal 1437 AH / January 2016 CE.

ISBN-10: 1-944781-88-9
ISBN-13: 9781944781880

Distributed by:

Salafi Publications
472 Coventry Road
Small Heath
Birmingham B10 0UG
United Kingdom

t. 0121 773 0033
e. admin@spubs.com

Germantown Masjid
4944 Germantown Avenue
Philadelphia
PA 19144
United States

t. 215 848 2615
e. admin@germantownmasjid.com

Website:

http://www.islamagainstextremism.com
iae@islamagainstextremism.com

Contents

Transliteration Table

The following tables provide the system of transliteration used for all non-translated Arabic terms appearing in this book.

Consonants

ء	ʾ	د	d	ض	ḍ	ك	k
ب	b	ذ	dh	ط	ṭ	ل	l
ت	t	ر	r	ظ	ẓ	م	m
ث	th	ز	z	ع	ʿ	ن	n
ج	j	س	s	غ	gh	ه	h
ح	ḥ	ش	sh	ف	f	و	w
خ	kh	ص	ṣ	ق	q	ي	y

Vowels

Short	ـَ	a	ـِ	i	ـُ	u
Long	ـَا	ā	ـِي	ī	ـُو	ū
Diphthongs	ـَوْ	aw	ـَيْ	ay		

Note:

1. All verses from the Qurʾān are approximate translations of its meanings. It is not possible to translate the Qurʾān into any other language whilst retaining its full depth and range of meaning.

2. Though the name of the creator in the Aramaic, Hebrew and Arabic languages is īl, eloh, ilāh, Allāh, "God" has been used throughout this work to make for easier reading for a non-Muslim audience.

In the name of God, the Most Merciful,
the Most Compassionate.

Introduction

This is a short guide aimed at helping non-Muslims of different beliefs and backgrounds to understand the foundations of Islām, what is required of Muslims by their faith and their duties towards non-Muslims and the societies within which they live. It addresses the historical foundations of the ideology of al-Qaeda and ISIS, the nature of the deviation of these groups and the Islāmic judgement regarding them. The views of al-Qaeda and ISIS ideologists on the "caliphate" and "jihād" are also analysed. In addition, parameters for identifying genuine signs of extremism as well as misinformation regarding Islām and Muslims have been presented. This information should enable the reader to recognise and be wary of hate propaganda spread by right-wing extremists and well-funded anti-Islām hate networks. To further their own political agendas, these groups use journalism, print and media to foster negativity and hatred against **one quarter of the world's population** – innocent, ordinary, peaceful Muslims going about their daily lives who despise and hate the terrorists as much as anyone else hates and despises them, if not more so.

It is hoped that greater awareness of Islām's stance on extremist ideology along with an accurate analysis of its true roots, causes and influences, will lead to credible measures being adopted to combat it effectively.

Abū ʿIyāḍ Amjad bin Muḥammad Rafīq
21 Rabīʿ al-Awwal 1437 / 1 January 2016

1. Does God Exist?

The question of God's existence would not ordinarily be addressed when explaining the foundations of Islām. Excessive confidence in conjectural, assumption-based sciences, a religious, dogmatic belief in materialist philosophy and the inability to make moral sense of the world in Western societies has given atheism a certain amount of traction. It is therefore worthwhile to present an answer to this question through one of numerous approaches. Research indicates that belief in a creator is innate and intuitive. Extensive indoctrination with materialist philosophy through primary, secondary and higher education is unable to remove the strong human tendency to see design and purpose in things. This tendency is very difficult to erase or override. Even atheists find it impossible to avoid the use of language which necessitates design and purpose in studies of the universe, phenomena and life.[1]

Those who deny the existence of a creator are largely driven by **psychological reasons**. They are unable to reconcile their perception and understanding of what takes place in the world with purposeful creation. Citing their inability to find the world morally intelligible, they feel uncomfortable that there should be an authority over the universe. This mental condition is known as **cosmic authority syndrome**. Highly credentialed, very smart atheists who have some honesty about them are not afraid to admit this. Thomas Nagel, an atheist philosopher, writes: "I want atheism to be true and am made uneasy by the fact that some of the most intelligent and well-informed people I know are religious believers. It isn't just that I don't believe in God and, naturally, hope that I'm right in my belief. It's that I hope there is no God! I don't want there to be a God; I don't want the universe to be like that. My guess is that this cosmic authority problem is not a rare condition..."[2]

---

[1] One can refer to these reports: "Humans May be Primed to Believe In Creation", New Scientist, 29 February 2009, and "Children are Born Believers in God", Daily Telegraph, 24 November 2008. Refer also to the article at http://aboutatheism.net/?zjggfhu which discusses research at Oxford University by Justin Barrett and Olivera Petrovich.

[2] In "The Last Word" (1997) p. 130-131. Nagel, **as an atheist**, is highly critical of the Darwinian materialist philosophy. He explains that its inability to explain consciousness, intentionality, meaning, or value is a major problem that has the capacity to undermine the entire naturalistic world picture. Refer to his

The not so honest atheists are unwilling to make this admission and present arguments which appear scientific and rational in order to convince people of alternative, **positively-asserted, religious beliefs**. These include: "creation by nothing" or "self-creation" or "life is purely accidental and purposeless". These are conjectures demanded by **a previous conviction** in materialist philosophy, propped up by theoretical, imaginary physics validated only by clever mathematics and not objective, empirical, scientific inquiry. No evidence exists to support these beliefs. They are simply preferred philosophical views. This is admitted by the more frank and honest atheists at the top of the hierarchy. The evolutionary biologist and atheist, Richard Lewontin writes: "It is not that the methods and institutions of science somehow compel us to accept a material explanation of the phenomenal world, but, on the contrary, that we are forced by our a priori adherence to material causes to create an apparatus of investigation and a set of concepts that produce material explanations, no matter how counter-intuitive, no matter how mystifying to the uninitiated. Moreover, that materialism is absolute, for we cannot allow a Divine Foot in the door."[3]

In other words: We have already decided that only material causes exist and have dismissed, from the outset, the existence of agency outside the universe before any science has been performed. We have constructed and organised the apparatus of science in such a way so that its conclusions can only be used to support this belief and none other. It is not that materialist philosophy is validated by science, we just don't feel comfortable with any other world view. Simply put, an atheist does not want God to exist and feels more comfortable emotionally without belief in God.

This **alternative competing belief system** (random, purposeless self-creation) is rejected by common sense, sensory perception, sound reason, self-evident truths and the sum of all human enterprise in the fields of industry, technology and biotechnology. Being able to observe and analyse the world around us, to make rational sense of it and the ability to innovate in many ways, industrially, technologically, biologically and biotechnologically through the understanding so

---

interesting book, "Mind and Cosmos: Why the Materialist Neo-Darwinian Conception of Nature is Almost Certainly False", Oxford Uni. Press, 2012.

[3] "Billions and Billions of Demons", New York Review, January 1997.

acquired – all of which demonstrates contrivance, order, organisation, intent, purpose, regularity, beauty and adaptation in what is being studied – is strong evidence of design and purpose in life and the universe. This leads to a warranted belief in a designer and maker.

A new field of science has emerged called **Biomimetics** or **Biomimicry** which is defined as the study and imitation of the models, systems, and elements of "nature" for the purpose of solving complex human problems. This indicates a number of things: First, it is impossible for anyone to study the universe and life without the assumption of design, regularity and order. Second, it is impossible to avoid the use of language that implies contrivance and design of a very complex nature in what is being studied. Third, in reproducing and mimicking this evident design in "nature", attributes such as knowledge, will, intent, power, purpose and wisdom are used by humans. It is rational, logical and warranted to assert that the same attributes are behind "nature", indicating that some sort of agency is involved. These simple, self-evident truths show why the vast majority of humans will never deviate from the strong, natural tendency to affirm a creator to account for the existence of the universe and life, despite sustained brainwashing with dogmatic materialist philosophy throughout the lifecycle of standard and higher education.[4]

---

[4] The objections of **David Hume** (d. 1776) in the 18th century were premature and were made at a time when designed artefacts were highly mechanical, machine-like and relatively crude. Hume would have found it difficult to make such objections in the 21st century and had naturalists and philosophers of centuries bygone known what is known today about the DNA-genome-cell system, it would only have solidified their belief in a creator and not provided any opportunity for conjectural materialist beliefs to take shape. The field of Biomimetics invalidates the bad analogy objection which asserts that man-made artefacts are unlike "natural" artefacts. The alternatives of "enough probable worlds" or "multiverses" to explain design are non-scientific attempts to escape from the obvious, innate, default position. The objection that the presence of evil, disease, harm and suffering indicates a less than perfect designer or multiple designers with conflicting goals is but a failure to understand the rules of the designer in his creation. It is merely an inability to grasp how effects are tied to causes and the laws of the creator with respect to his creation. This knowledge cannot be reached by philosophers and scientists and is the reason why philosophers, scientists and atheists cannot provide any logical, rational basis for morality. Hence, this objection does not affect the validity of the foundation of the argument itself. Finally, the objection of the

From this brief discussion, belief in a creator is innate, natural, rational, warranted, and according to research is like a seed planted in the heart, soul and mind of every human from birth which cannot be easily erased. In light of this, Islām is best viewed as something that nourishes this seed to bring about the fruits of perfection in human morals and character.

2. What is Islām?

The word Islām means the attainment of **inner satisfaction**, **peace** and **serenity** and **outward perfection in character** through the submission of one's will to God in pure monotheism. It is founded upon the firm belief that there is no being or thing which deserves to be worshipped but God alone. As mentioned previously, research indicates that every child is born with an inherent capacity to affirm the existence of a creator through the simplest of observations.[5] If left alone without any instruction or contrary teaching, a child will develop a natural desire to show gratitude to this creator for the very apparent favours and bounties experienced and enjoyed in life. This natural inclination is the seed referred to earlier and is known as **fiṭrah** in Islāmic terminology. It predisposes an individual to recognise and accept the message of the prophets of God such as Abraham, Moses, Jesus and Muḥammad which only has one name: Islām.

These prophets never called to mere belief in God, as this is innate and self-evident, but they called to worshipping God alone and prohibited the worshipping of stones, idols, statues, trees, the Earth, sun, moon and other heavenly bodies. They also prohibited the worship of human beings such as saints, the righteous living or dead and the prophets themselves. Likewise, they prohibited from taking the various elements and forces or anything from the system of "natural" causes and effects as deities, since worshipping them, instead of or alongside the one who placed them, is futile and opposes reason. They

---

designer requiring a designer and hence an infinite regress of designers is baseless because by definition, God is uncreated and therefore eternal.

[5] Based on research at Oxford University by Justin Barrett and Olivera Petrovich and refer also to "Humans May be Primed to Believe in Creation", New Scientist, 29 February 2009, and "Children Are Born Believers in God", Daily Telegraph, 24 November 2008.

also prohibited superstition and believing things to be causes of effects that they have no connection to. These are doorways to false beliefs about the creation and lead to baseless and potentially harmful actions. All the prophets of God came with this central, uniform message of **pure monotheism** in belief, word and deed. Anyone who affirms this belief and accepts all the messengers of God without exception and without distinguishing between them has established the first pillar of Islām and is a Muslim.

Thereafter, observant Muslims perform **daily prayers** in a state of physical cleanliness as a form of devotion and gratitude to God for his innumerable favours. They **fast** by refraining from food and drink from dawn to sunset during the month of Ramaḍān as a means of exercising patience and developing sympathy for the hungry. They give **obligatory charity** to the poor and needy from their excess wealth. If they have financial ability and the means, they make **pilgrimage** to Mecca, the place where Abraham built the place of God's worship known as the Kaʿbah. These are the **five pillars** of Islām: The testimony that none has the right to worship but God alone, the five daily prayers, fasting the month of Ramaḍān, giving obligatory charity and making pilgrimage to Mecca if one has the ability to do so. Building on top of the five pillars, a Muslim fulfils the most emphatic obligations which include: Honouring parents and lowering the wing of humility to them, benevolence to relatives and honouring neighbours whether Muslim or non-Muslim. Likewise, being truthful in speech and deed, fulfilling promises, abiding by contracts, shunning treachery in all its forms and withholding from injustice against others irrespective of whether they are Muslims or non-Muslims.

God stated in the Qurʾān: "**And your Lord has decreed that you do not worship except Him alone, and to parents, good treatment... Lower the wing of humility and mercy to them and say, 'O My Lord, show mercy to them as they [showed mercy] to me when bringing me up'**." (17:23-24). And: "**Establish the daily prayer and give the obligatory charity**." (2:110). And: "**Verily, God commands with justice, good conduct, and giving to relatives**." (16:90). And, "**O you who believe, fulfill all contracts**." (5:1). And: "**O my people, give full weight and measure in justice**." (11:85). And: "**O you who believe, fear God and speak upright words of truth and justice**." (33:70). And: "**O you who believe, fear God and be with those who are truthful**." (9:119). The Prophet (peace be upon him) said in a famous tradition: "Whoever believes in God and the final day (of reckoning), let him honour his neighbour." And in another authentic tradition: "By God, he does not have faith, by God, he does not have faith, by God, he does not have faith whose neighbour is not safe from his harm." He also said: "Three are the signs of a hypocrite: When he speaks he lies, when he makes a promise he breaks it and when he is trusted he acts treacherously." He also said: "Beware of oppression, for oppression will be layers of darkness on the Day of Judgement." He also said: "Verily, whoever oppressed a non-Muslim under covenant, cheated him, burdened him over his capacity or took something from him which he did not willingly give, then I will be his disputant on the Day of Judgement."

As for **perfection of character**, this was the purpose of the Prophet's mission. He stated in a famous authentic tradition: "I have not been sent except for the completion of noble manners." He also said: "The most perfect of believers in faith are those with the best manners and the best of you are those who are best to their women." The Qur'ān and the Prophetic traditions are replete with calls for Muslims to adorn themselves with the loftiest of qualities which include sincerity, humility, patience, piety, charity, forgiveness, forbearance, compassion, justice, trustworthiness and honesty. The pagans of Mecca acknowledged the virtuous, superior character of the Prophet (peace be upon him) and could not fault him in that regard, despite being staunch enemies.

The standard of character demanded by Islām is so great that many notable righteous Muslim scholars in history were highly praised by Christians and Jews. By way of example, Imām Aḥmad bin Ḥanbal (d. 855), one of the greatest scholars of early Islām was treated by a Christian physician once. When the Christian entered upon him, he said: "I have desired to see you for many years. Your presence is not only rectification for the people of Islām, but for the whole of creation. There is to be found none amongst our Christian associates except that he is pleased with you."[6]

Regretfully, many Muslims have abandoned the upright guidance whose beneficial and positive effects bring this type of recognition and honour. They have become, as the Prophet himself stated, "like the froth of the ocean".

---

[6] In the Musnad of Imām Aḥmad (p. 79) with checking of Aḥmad Shākir.

3. What is the Qur'ān?

Islāmic teachings are derived from two primary sources. The first is the Qur'ān. Muslims believe that the Qur'ān is the actual spoken word of God conveyed by Gabriel to Muḥammad in the clear Arabic language. Unlike the Torah and the Gospel, the Qur'ān comprises only the word of God. It is not a mixture of the word of God, the word of the Prophet and the words of his disciples. It consists of 114 chapters varying in length. Whole chapters, passages or individual verses were revealed to Prophet Muḥammad over a period of twenty-three years in relation to incidents and occurrences.

These revelations were written down and memorised by his companions who also knew the context of revelation for each verse or passage. Prior to Islām the Arabs were illiterate and did not used to write. However, they were masters of language and the art of oratory. They had developed superb memories, could recite thousands of verses of poetry from memory and frequently engaged in "poetic warfare" with their opponents. When the Qur'ān was revealed, its recital mesmerised listeners and began winning and captivating hearts, taking the pagan Arabs by surprise. They were challenged to produce something like it in its meanings, style, eloquence and power but were unable. They could not believe they had been surpassed in the art of expression and rendered incapable. This led them to make various accusations against the Prophet. God said: "**And it was not [possible] for this Qur'ān to be produced by other than God, but [it is] a confirmation of what was before it and a detailed explanation of the [former] Scripture, about which there is no doubt, from the Lord of the worlds**." (10:37). The Qur'ān was memorised by thousands of the Prophet's companions and was conveyed in both oral and written form through successive transmission on such a large scale not known for any other book in history. If every single copy of the Qur'ān was removed from the Earth at night, the Muslims would have it written down from memory by the next morning. The Qur'ān describes itself as **light** (nūr), **mercy** (raḥmah) **guidance** (hudā), **healing** (shifā') an **admonition** (maw'iẓah), a **criterion** (furqān), a **reminder** (dhikr), **wise** (ḥakīm), **the best of speech** (aḥsan al-kalām) amongst many other descriptions. It summarises its objective in one sentence, "**Verily, this Qur'ān guides to that which is upright and best**." (17:9).

4. What is the Sunnah?

The Sunnah is the second of the two primary sources. It refers to the authentic Prophetic traditions in which the sayings and actions of the Prophet have been preserved. These traditions provide the basis for correctly interpreting the Qurʾān. The Prophet not only conveyed the Qurʾān with integrity, he also provided its explanation through his sayings and actions. His companions memorised and preserved these traditions by conveying them to their own students. They were written down and later codified and organised into compilations which became standard references for studying the Prophetic traditions. An unequalled, rigorous scientific system known as **The Science of Report Transmission** (ʿilm al-ḥadīth) was developed through the efforts of Muslim scholars who collected these traditions to ensure that nothing false was attributed to the Prophet (peace be upon him) for he had warned: "Whoever said upon me that which I did not say, let him find his place in the Hellfire." The Prophet's teachings are preserved through the highest standards of oral transmission ever known in the history of mankind. The Muslim nation was given the **chain of narration** (isnād)[7] and the rigorous science associated with it is unparallelled and unmatched in history.

---

[7] The word isnād means ascription and refers to the chain of authorities through whom the Prophetic traditions were transmitted and collected. It is a complex, highly-developed, rigorous science. No nation prior to the Islāmic nation was given such a science to aid in the preservation of revealed knowledge. Without preservation of the Prophetic traditions, explanation of the Qurʾān and extraction of legal rulings would not be possible and the religion would have been distorted and wasted. ʿAbdullāh bin al-Mubārak (d. 797) said: "The isnād is from the religion, had it not been for the isnād, anyone could have said what he willed." Related by the famous Imām Muslim bin al-Ḥajjāj in his introduction to his collection of Prophetic traditions. European Orientalists who began to study Islām over the past few centuries have tried to undermine this system as part of a broader objective to weaken Islāmic sciences. However their ignorance of the sophistication and depth of this science, studying it as unqualified outsiders interested only in undermining the science and not understanding it objectively, left them in a hapless state with glaring contradictions in their theories and claims. A large body of literature exists comprising a robust, powerful response by competent Muslim authorities in this regard.

Unlike the Torah and the Gospel which contain a confusing mixture of what is ascribed to God, the sayings of the prophets, and the sayings of the mostly unidentified scribes who penned the various books comprising the Torah and the Gospel, the Qurʾān and the Sunnah are distinct. There is no confusion between the words of the Prophet and the words of his companions and disciples, let alone confusion between the words of God and the words of the Prophet.

5. How do Muslims interpret their primary sources?

The correct understanding and implementation of these two primary sources have been safeguarded and conveyed by the Prophet's disciples and companions. They are the criterion between correct and false interpretations of primary texts and their statements have been recorded and preserved for those after them. This means that not only do the Islāmic sources have textual integrity, they also have a standard of interpretation through which controversies can be resolved and deviations can be identified. The presence of different Muslim sects where each one claims to be following primary sources is due to misinterpretation, abandoning the understanding of the Prophet's companions and relying upon opinions, tastes and desires. In contrast to the original messages of Moses and Jesus which have been altered and lost, **the Islāmic sources have both textual and interpretive integrity**. This means that the original message is always accessible for the one who desires and pursues it. Further, universal principles have been laid down in the primary texts which allow legal rulings to be derived for new situations and circumstances not addressed directly by the texts. Muslim scholars of each era can return to these principles and with the use of sound analogy (qiyās), determine rulings.

Due to the exact nature of the sciences related to the Qurʾān and the Prophetic traditions and the presence of a standard of interpretation, it is not possible for anyone to attempt to misrepresent any aspect of Islām without some or all of the scholars of the Muslims who adhere to the original guidance being able to expose his error in a rigorous scientific manner. For example, the first sect to break away from Islām, the Khārijites (extremist renegades), misinterpreted the Qurʾān. Their deviation in this interpretation has been on the record for 1400 years ever since Ibn ʿAbbās, the Prophet's cousin and expert scholar of the Qurʾān, refuted them. It is why throughout the centuries, one can find robust and decisive rebuttals against their ideology in the works of Muslim scholars.

6. Who was Muḥammad?

Muḥammad[8] (d. 632) was the son of ʿAbdullāh, the son of ʿAbd al-Muṭṭalib, the son of Hāshim and his lineage traces back, through twenty-one generations, to ʿAdnān who was from the offspring of Ismāʿīl, the son of Abraham. The lineage of his mother, ʾĀminah, also traces back to Abraham through a common ancestor. He was sent at a time when the civilisations of the world had departed from the teachings of their respective messengers. The Jews and Christians had strayed from the messages of Moses and Jesus and altered the Torah and the Gospel. The pagan Arabs had abandoned the religion of Abraham and turned to the worship of numerous deities besides God. It was an era in human history when most of the people of the Earth had turned to the worship of the elements, forces, stones, trees, idols, statues, heavenly bodies, the righteous dead and even the prophets themselves. They were engrossed in superstition, oppression and exploitation. Every nation had been sent a messenger calling them to single out God with worship as mentioned in the Qurʾān: "**We indeed raised amongst every nation a messenger [with the message]: Worship God alone and shun false deities.**" (16:36), but this message had been distorted and lost. Muḥammad (peace be upon him) was sent to affirm this message and present it in a detailed, comprehensive form that was to remain preserved in both its text and interpretation.

For thirteen years in Mecca, the Prophet preached peacefully to the pagan Arabs. He invited them to single out God in worship and shun the worship of deities that are powerless over benefit or harm. He spoke against their racism, their maltreatment of slaves, killing of female newborns and other misdeeds. He enjoined benevolence to widows and orphans and the frequent giving of charity. Unfortunately,

---

[8] The name "Muḥammad" means "praised." His mention has been made explicitly in the Hebrew Torah of Moses as "Muḥammad" (מחמד) and in the Aramaic Gospel of Jesus as "Aḥmad" (אחמד) which means "most praised." Muḥammad is the most mentioned and praised man on Earth. He is praised for his lofty characteristics and virtues. However, he is not worshipped.

his message was not in the personal, economic and political interests of the pagans of Mecca. He was met with hostility and his believing companions were oppressed, tortured and murdered. Attempts were made on his life and he was forced to migrate to what became known as the city of Medina. He continued preaching whilst facing hostility, plots, intrigues and the machinations of the polytheists and various forces who formed alliances and initiated wars against him.

Being granted permission to ward off aggression and injustice from himself and his believing companions, he only fought to defend the instrument of peaceful preaching so that the message of Islām, genuine monotheism and perfection of human morals and character, could be heard by others without hindrance. He never forced a single person to accept Islām against his will. As the Muslim scholar, **Ibn al-Qayyim** (d. 1350) pointed out: "It will become clear to whoever reflects upon the biographical account of the Prophet (peace be upon him) that he did not compel a single person to accept his religion, ever. Rather, he fought whoever fought against him [first]."[9] One will be surprised to learn that in the eight years from 622 to 630, there were no more than around 800 to 900 deaths in all the various wars that the Prophet participated in. Further, these wars were not initiated by him but were in response to unjustified aggression towards his peaceful activities. Honest historians make note of this fact. **Lawrence Browne** wrote: "Incidentally these well-established facts dispose of the idea so widely fostered in Christian writings that the Muslims, wherever they went, forced people to accept Islam at the point of the sword."[10] **James Michener** wrote: "No other religion in history spread so rapidly as Islam. The West has widely believed that this surge of religion was made possible by the sword. But no modern scholar accepts this idea."[11] **De Lacy O'Leary** wrote: "History makes it clear, however, that the legend of fanatical Muslims sweeping through the world and forcing Islam at the point of sword upon conquered races is one of the most fantastically absurd myths that historians have ever repeated."[12]

The 19th and early 20th centuries were a period of time in which researchers, academics and notable figures in the West were

[9] "Hidāyat al-Ḥayārā", Dār ʿĀlam al-Fawāʾid, pp. 29-30.
[10] "The Prospects of Islām", 1944.
[11] "Reader's Digest", May 1955, pp. 68-70.
[12] "Islam at the Crossroads", London, 1923.

beginning to overcome medieval prejudices against Islām and objectively study the life of the Prophet (peace be upon him). One can find many statements from this period in which the Prophet is praised by for his virtuous qualities and great achievements. **Washington Irving** (d. 1859), American author and diplomat, wrote: "He was sober and abstemious in his diet, and a rigorous observer of fasts. He indulged in no magnificence of apparel, the ostentation of a petty mind; neither was his simplicity in dress affected, but the result of a real disregard to distinction from so trivial a source... In his private dealings he was just. He treated friends and strangers, the rich and poor, the powerful and the weak, with equity, and was beloved by the common people for the affability with which he received them, and listened to their complaints... His military triumphs awakened no pride nor vain glory, as they would have done had they been effected for selfish purposes. In the time of his greatest power he maintained the same simplicity of manners and appearance as in the days of his adversity. So far from affecting regal state, he was displeased if, on entering a room, any unusual testimonial of respect were shown to him."[13] **William Montgomery Watt** (d. 2006), Professor (Emeritus) of Arabic and Islāmic Studies at the University of Edinburgh, wrote: "His readiness to undergo persecutions for his beliefs, the high moral character of the men who believed in him and looked up to him as leader, and the greatness of his ultimate achievement – all argue his fundamental integrity. To suppose Muḥammad an impostor[14] raises more problems than it solves. Moreover, none of the great figures of history is so poorly appreciated in the West as Muḥammad."[15] **Ramakrishna Rao**, Hindu professor of Philosophy writes: "The personality of Muḥammad, it is most difficult to get into the whole truth of it. Only a glimpse of it I can catch. What a dramatic succession of picturesque scenes. There is Muḥammad the Prophet. There is Muḥammad the Warrior; Muḥammad the Businessman; Muḥammad the Statesman; Muḥammad the Orator; Muḥammad the Reformer; Muḥammad the Refuge of Orphans; Muḥammad the Protector of

---

[13] "Life of Mahomet", London, 1889, pp. 192-3, 199.

[14] Montgomery Watt has indicated here the problem that many Orientalists and academics encounter when they question the integrity of the Prophet in their writings.

[15] "Mohammad at Mecca", Oxford, 1953, p. 52.

Slaves; Muḥammad the Emancipator of Women; Muḥammad the Judge; Muḥammad the Saint.[16] All in all these magnificent roles, in all these departments of human activities, he is like a hero."[17]

John William Draper, (d. 1882), American scientist, philosopher, and historian, wrote: "Four years after the death of Justinian, A.D. 569, was born at Mecca, in Arabia the man who, of all men, exercised the greatest influence upon the human race... Moḥammed."[18] **Alphonse de Lamartine** (d. 1869), French poet and statesman, wrote: "Philosopher,[19] orator, apostle, legislator, warrior, conqueror of ideas, restorer of rational dogmas, of a cult without images; the founder of twenty terrestrial empires and of one spiritual empire, that is Muḥammad. As regards all standards by which human greatness may be measured, we may well ask, is there any man greater than he?"[20] **Edward Gibbon** (d. 1794), the famous British historian, wrote: "The greatest success of Moḥammad's life was effected by sheer moral force without the stroke of a sword."[21] **Annie Besant** (d. 1933), British socialist, wrote: "It is impossible for anyone who studies the life and character of the great Prophet of Arabia, who knows how he taught and how he lived, to feel anything but reverence for that mighty Prophet, one of the great messengers of the Supreme. And although in what I put to you I shall say many things which may be familiar to many, yet I myself feel whenever I re-read them, a new way of admiration, a new sense of reverence for that mighty Arabian teacher."[22] **David George Hogarth** (d. 1927), English archaeologist author and keeper of the Ashmolean Museum, Oxford, wrote: "Serious or trivial, his daily

---

[16] In Islām the concepts of "sainthood" or "holiness" do not exist. These are Christian concepts comprising exaggeration which lead to worship of men.

[17] In his work, "Muḥammad the Prophet of Islām."

[18] "A History of the Intellectual Development of Europe", 1875, vol.1, pp. 329-330. Draper's view is also expressed by others who list the Prophet as the most influential man in history, above all other famous people, be they kings, philosophers, leaders, reformists, scientists or religious figures.

[19] Muḥammad (peace be upon him) was not a philosopher. His teachings were not his own opinions or reasoning. Rather, his speech was revelation inspired by God. Even the pagan Arabs, **masters of oratory**, were unable to confute him and rival the Qur'ān that was revealed to him.

[20] A translated excerpt from "Histoire De La Turquie", Paris, 1854.

[21] "History of The Saracen Empire", London, 1870.

[22] "The Life And Teachings Of Muhammad", Madras, 1932, p. 4.

behaviour has instituted a canon which millions observe this day with conscious mimicry. No one regarded by any section of the human race as Perfect Man has been imitated so minutely. The conduct of the founder of Christianity has not so governed the ordinary life of His followers. Moreover, no founder of a religion has been left on so solitary an eminence as the Muslim Apostle."[23] **Gustav Weil** (d. 1889), German scholar, wrote: "His house, his dress, his food – they were characterized by a rare simplicity. So unpretentious was he that he would receive from his companions no special mark of reverence, nor would he accept any service from his slave which he could do himself. Often and often indeed he was seen in the market purchasing provisions; often and often was he seen mending his clothes in his room, or milking a goat in his courtyard. He was accessible to all, and at all times and whenever politics was not in the way, he was generous and forbearing to a degree. Unlimited was his benevolence and generosity, and so was his anxious care for the welfare of the community."[24]

Despite the many wars of aggression waged to extinguish his message, the Prophet came out victorious and the entire Arabian peninsula entered Islām during the last two years of his life, willingly and without compulsion. The majority of its inhabitants had been waiting in anticipation to see which of the two factions – the Prophet and his followers or the Meccans and their numerous allies – would come out victorious, upon their conviction that God would not give victory and custody of Mecca to a liar. When the Prophet conquered Mecca peacefully and spared its 10,000 inhabitants, showing his great mercy and clemency, people rushed to accept Islām out of choice.

7. How do Muslims view Moses and Jesus?

Muslims believe in all the prophets and messengers of God and do not make distinctions between them. From the greatest, most resolute of messengers are Moses and Jesus (peace be upon them both). **Moses** is mentioned **124 times** by name in the Qur'ān, more than any other prophet of God. **Jesus** is mentioned around **twenty times**. All the prophets and messengers were humble, honest, righteous men.

---

[23] In his book, "Arabia", Oxford, 1922, p. 52

[24] "A History of the Islāmic Peoples", English translation, 1914, pp. 27-28.

They did not possess any attribute of divinity, nor did they ever claim to. Nor did they call people to worship them. They preached the message of Islām and invited to genuine, pure monotheism. If one was to investigate the language of Moses, Jesus and Muḥammad, one will find identical phraseology in explanation of the message they called to. This is because the languages of Hebrew, Aramaic and Arabic are very closely related. The words **ilāh**, **elohim**, **Allāh** (the one true deity), **salām** (peace), **Islām** (submission), **muslim** (submitter) and the concept of **tawḥīd** (monotheism) were used by these prophets in conveying their message. Hence, Moses was a Muslim, as were all the prophets of the Children of Israel (Banī Isrā'īl) including Solomon, David, Jesus and John. Islām was the name of their religion. God said: **"Say: The way acceptable to God is Islām. But those who were given the Book did not differ except out of envy, after knowledge had come to them.**" (3:19). Traces of this message of Islām can be found in what remains of the Torah and the Gospel.[25] In Deuteronomy 6:4 we find: "Hear O Israel, the Lord our God, the Lord is one." And in Mark 12:29: "'The most important one,' answered Jesus, 'is this: 'Hear, O Israel: The Lord our God, the Lord is one'." The meaning is lost in translation, but these statements, in the original Hebrew or Aramaic (יְהוָה אֱלֹהֵינוּ, יְהוָה אֶחָד) and (יְהוָה אֶחָד וּשְׁמוֹ אֶחָד) would be identical to the statement **ilāhunā aḥād** – "Our Lord and Deity is uniquely one" – and **qul huwallāhu aḥad** – "Say: He is Allāh [who is] Uniquely One" – and the declaration of monotheism in Islām, **lā ilāha illallāh,** which means: "None has the right to be worshipped but God alone." Muslims

[25] Muslims hold that the Torah and the Gospel have undergone alteration and distortion over time and are no longer accurate representations of what God revealed to Moses and Jesus. Rebuking the Jews and Christians, God stated: "**So woe to those who write the 'scripture' with their own hands, then say, 'This is from God' in order to exchange it for a small price. Woe to them for what their hands have written and woe to them for what they earn thereby**." (2:79). And also: "**And indeed, there is among them a party who alter the Scripture with their tongues so you may think it is from the Scripture, but it is not from the Scripture. And they say, 'This is from God,' but it is not from God. And they speak a lie against God while they know**." (3:78). We find in the Book of Jeremiah in the Old Testament: "How can you say, 'We are wise, for we have the law of the Lord,' when actually the lying pen of the scribes has handled it falsely?" (Jeremiah 8:8). This indicates that tampering with Scripture was a known matter in that time and was documented within the very Scripture itself.

consider all of the Prophets sent by God as brothers who preached the same message.

As for what is known as Judaism today, Muslims believe it is not what Moses originally called to. Judaism is named after the tribe of Judah, one of the twelve tribes of Israel.[26] The Jewish Encyclopedia[27] makes a distinction between the original Mosaic teachings and **Rabbinic Judaism**, a later development which has remained the main character of Judaism till today. In fact, the Jewish Encylopedia mentions that Judaism underwent frequent changes throughout the ages. It was strongly affected and moulded by the beliefs and practices of host nations such as Egypt, Persia and Babylonia.

The Qurʾān rehearsed to Jews in the era of Muḥammad (peace be upon him) the great favours God had bestowed upon them when they had been upon right guidance and were the best of nations. It reminded them how their religious leaders had departed from the guidance of Moses, altered their scripture and law, entered into the practice of sorcery, fell into polytheism, contended with their prophets and distorted the religion of Islām.

The religious elders who resided in Babylon from the 6th century BC onwards authored a new doctrine based upon race, nationality and land. They weaved it into their writings of the books of the Old Testament and also developed an oral tradition which later became the Talmud. Despite claims of adherence to monotheism, this oral tradition was a mixture of the dictates of religious leaders, occultism, gnostic-spirituality, magic and the shackles of invented observances, statutes and laws that became the basis for a despotic micro-management by religious leaders of the lives of ordinary Jews. It superseded the original Torah given to Moses, though it is claimed to be an elaboration of it. In Rabbinic Judaism, religious leaders assume divine authority, claiming God continues to speak and reveal to them. Jesus (peace be upon him) was sent to revive the religion of Islām brought by Moses and to purify and confirm his law which had been altered. The Pharisees who were the elitist religious elders of the time rejected his call and resented their authority being undermined. Jesus's opposition

---

[26] Muslim exegetes of the Qurʾān have affirmed the meaning of the Hebrew word "Israel" as "Slave of God", a title of Prophet Jacob (peace be upon him).

[27] "The Jewish Encyclopedia", 1906, 7/359 under the entry of "Judaism."

to them and his repudiation of the "traditions of the elders" which were their inventions and additions brought him scorn and plots were hatched against him. Although he was granted many miracles as proof that he was a genuine prophet, this only earned him the accusation of sorcery and idolatry. He was subsequently depicted in Talmudic literature as a madman, idolater and sorcerer[28] and his mother, Mary (peace be upon her) was reviled and accused of enormous things. In reality, his mother was a chaste, righteous woman. Jesus was given a miraculous birth and was sent as a prophet of God to the Children of Israel and the House of Judah. He called to genuine monotheism and came to confirm the law of Moses and guide the "Lost Sheep of the House of Israel".

In the 13th century after Jesus another part of the secretive, exclusive oral tradition, referred to as the **Qabbalah** (a system of "magic" for the invocation of spirits and forces presented as mysticism) was put into writing in the form of the Zohar and penetrated the various centres of Judaism across the world until it became mainstream. This system of magic incorporated an emanationist, pantheistic type of philosophy wherein Rabbis became God on Earth and were alleged to effect change in the universe through their supernatural powers. This religion known as **Rabbinic Judaism** or **Classic Judaism** formed after the destruction of the temple in 70 CE. Its nucleus – "the traditions of the elders" in the form of the Talmūd and the Qabbalah, centred around a tribal doctrine – is not the religion of Islām brought by Moses and the rest of the Israelite prophets.[29]

---

[28] Refer to the work of Peter Schäfer, Professor of Judaic Studies, titled "Jesus in the Talmud", Princeton University Press, 2009. A summary of the depiction of Jesus in Talmudic literature is that Jesus was guilty of falsehood and heresy, born an illegitimate child of an immoral woman, foolish and insane, a conjurer and a magician, an idolater, a seducer with "an eye for the ladies", killed and crucified for his crimes and immersed in boiling excrement in Hellfire. Muslims vehemently reject this view as baseless, just as they vehemently reject the deification and worship of Jesus as baseless.

[29] Israel Shahak points out that modern **Orthodox Judaism** is a direct continuation of classical **Rabbinic Judaism** and has been taken over completely by the Qabbalic system of magic in virtually all of its centres. Refer to "Jewish History, Jewish Religion", Pluto Press, 2008, pp. 38-39. One can also refer to the following useful resources: "Roots of Rabbinic Judaism: An Intellectual History from Ezekiel to Daniel" by Gabriele Boccaccini, Erdmans,

As for Christianity, it is based upon **beliefs about Jesus** but not upon the actual **beliefs of Jesus**. The earliest believers in Jesus were Israelites. They included the Ebionites and numerous other sects. However, Paul (Saul of Tarsus) opposed the true disciples of Jesus who were loyal to his teachings and invented a new mythical Jesus for the Greeks and Romans in line with their existing belief systems. The authors of the gospels then weaved Paul's ideas in their writings (in Greek). Later, Constantine (d. 337), the Roman Emperor and leader in the sun-worshipping cult known as **Sol Invictus** (Invincible Sun), absorbed Christianity into Roman paganism as a means of power consolidation in his empire. Whereas in the pure Gospel of Jesus, God was one, without partners and to be worshipped alone to the exclusion of all other deities coupled with adherence to the law, a Pauline Greco-Roman framing of the Israelite Prophet and Messiah, brought a Christianity for "Gentiles" no different to the mystery-religions they were already upon: **belief in human gods, incarnations, saviours, sacrifices, redemptions and rebirths**. As Christianity spread through Europe with the force of empire, additional pagan concepts and rituals were absorbed. The innovated Trinity itself did not receive a complete formulation until after ongoing disputes and many councils, the last of them, the Council of Chalcedon being held in 451 CE.

In short, when the message of Jesus was taken to the pagans of the Mediterranean, the mythology of those civilizations was weaved and incorporated into the message, thereby obliterating the original message. Concepts of trinity, begotten son, sun-god, resurrection, rebirth and redemption were already widespread during that era with respect to the deities of the Egyptians, Greeks, Persians, and Romans such as Osiris, Horus, Isis, Mithra, Dionysus, Attis and Bāl. Constantine, the pagan Roman emperor, imposed his version of 'Christianity' as the state religion after an apparent 'conversion'.[30] Jesus was deified and worshipped alongside God. It became more or less impossible for any 'Christian' to know and practice the true way of Jesus a couple of centuries after him.

2001, and "Rabbinic Judaism" by Jacob Neusner and William Scott Green, Fortress Press, 1995.

[30] Historical and archaeological evidence shows that Constantine remained a practising pagan. Today's 'Christianity' is Pauline Greco-Roman Christianity and is far removed from the original pure monotheistic message of Jesus.

The only way 'Christians' today can follow the message of Jesus is by following the final Messenger, Muḥammad who was sent with a perfection of the Islām brought by the previous prophets of God. Muḥammad (peace be upon him) said: "Both in this world and the next, I am the nearest of all the people to Jesus, son of Mary, and all the prophets are paternal brothers, and there has been no prophet between me and him (Jesus)."[31] He also said: "Whoever testifies that no deity is worthy of worship but God alone, without any partners, that Muḥammad is His servant and Messenger, that Jesus is the servant of God, His Word which He bestowed upon Mary, a Spirit from Him, and that Paradise is true and Hellfire is true, then he will enter Paradise through any of the eight gates of Paradise he wishes."[32] God said in the Qur'ān: "**O People of the Scripture, do not commit excess in your religion or say about God except the truth. The Messiah, Jesus, the son of Mary, was but a messenger of God and His word which He directed to Mary and a soul [created at a command] from Him. So believe in God and His messengers. And do not say, 'Three'. Desist, it is better for you. Indeed, God is but one deity. Exalted is He above having a son. To Him belongs whatever is in the heavens and whatever is on the earth. And sufficient is God as Disposer of affairs**."(4:79).[33]

---

[31] Reported by Imām al-Bukhāri in his Ṣaḥīḥ.

[32] Reported by Imām Muslim in his Ṣaḥīh

[33] The Islāmic commentators of the Qur'ān provided this elaboration of the meaning of the verse: O people of the Gospel, do not exceed the true belief and do not exaggerate and say of God except the truth. Do not claim a son for God, for Jesus the son of Mary was no more than a messenger like many other messengers before him. He was commanded to shun all other deities, worship God alone, submit to His will and observe the law. Jesus is the Messenger of God. He is the Word of God, with the meaning that he was created through a Word spoken by God which is "Be!" – not that he, Jesus, in his essence, is the actual Word of God. It was through this Word that Gabriel was sent and he breathed from the Spirit (Rūḥ) of God into Mary. The Spirit is not a part of God's essence but a created entity which gives rise to life and its reality is unknown. The same Spirit was breathed into Ādam who was born without father and mother. Through this Spirit came the miraculous birth of Jesus. Hence, Jesus is the Word and the Spirit of God. He was created through God's Word of command and the sending and breathing of the created Spirit through Gabriel. So people of the Gospel, believe in this truth regarding Jesus, the Son of Mary and submit to God alone. Shun the worship of all other deities including Jesus

Muslims have been ordered to engage with Jews and Christians with dialogue and good admonition: "**Say: 'O People of the Book, come to a word that is just between us and you: That we worship none but God, that we associate no partners with Him, and that none of us shall take others as lords besides God. But if they turn away, then say, 'Bear witness that we are Muslims [submitting to Him]'.**" (3:64). "**And do not argue with the People of the Book except in a way that is best.**" (29:46).

8. What are the roots of the ideology of the terrorists?

It is not possible to fully grasp the true nature and reality al-Qaeda and ISIS without looking at how their ideology first appeared at the dawn of Islām. This ideology first arose as a war against Islām, its leaders, its people and the lands inhabited by them and can be seen in no other way. From the details and analysis to follow, the erroneous attempts to ascribe this ideology to even "fundamentalist" or "conservative" Islām, let alone Islām itself, will become readily apparent. This has been alluded to by the **French Professor Olivier Roy** whose statement in this regard is cited later in this work.

In the year 630 CE, whilst the Prophet (peace be upon him) was distributing charities to certain remote tribes to show benevolence to them, a group of people from his own region were disgruntled about not receiving any share. Their leader and spokesman, known as **Dhul-Khuwaiṣirah al-Tamīmī**, ordered the Prophet to be just and accused him of judging by personal interests. This amounted to accusing the Prophet of not judging by God's law, which commands justice in all dealings. The Qurʾān revealed these people to be hypocrites who made only an outward display of Islām, did not possess genuine

---

and his mother Mary and do not say "There are three (deities)", for there is only one deity worthy of worship in truth. You have unjustly raised Jesus from the station of prophethood and messengership to one of lordship (rubūbiyyah). Yet Jesus and his mother Mary were mere mortals, they ate, drank and walked the Earth and owned and controlled nothing in the heavens and Earth, save that God bestowed miracles upon Jesus as a sign of his prophethood. Desist from this statement of "Three", believe in the absolute oneness of God and worship only Him alone. This is the straight path indicated by authentic, uncorrupted revelation and sound reason.

internal faith and were motivated by the world. Muḥammad (peace be upon him) prophesized that through the main spokesman of this group and his ideas **an insurgent group** will appear and referred to them as **Khārijites** (extremist renegades).

He prophesized that they will revolt against the Muslims and their leaders. He explained that they will display much outward piety in terms of abundant worship, fasting and recitation of the Qur'ān, however, this worship would be outwardly only, without it touching their hearts. He said that the Qur'ān would not go beyond their throats. He described them as young in age, foolish-minded individuals who will strive to kill the people of Islām. He also informed his companions of the direction of their appearance which would be to the east, in Irāq. He also prophesized that a revolutionary group will contend with the third caliph 'Uthmān (d. 656) for leadership and murder him in the process. Likewise, he prophesized that his cousin and son-in-law, **'Alī bin Abī Ṭālib** (d. 661) would fight and defeat this renegade group during a time of civil strife where the main body of the Muslims will have split into two. He also prophesized that they will continue to appear and rise against the Muslim nation throughout the ages – killing the people of Islām with much bloodshed – until the Anti-Christ[34] will appear in the midst of their armies in the later times.

The Prophet spoke of them and their traits using extremely harsh words, indicating the severity of their misguidance and the great corruption and harm they would bring to the world. In numerous authentic traditions which are well-known and famous, he said of them: **"They recite the Qur'ān but it does not pass beyond their throats."**, **"They exit from Islām as swiftly as the arrow passes straight through its target."**, **"They are the worst of creation."**, **"They are the worst of those killed beneath the canopy of the sky."**, **"They are the Dogs of Hellfire."**, **"If I was to reach them, I would slaughter them, like the slaughtering of 'Ād."**[35], **"Kill them wherever you find them for there is a reward for the one who kills them."**, **"They will not cease to appear until the last of them**

---

[34] Muslims believe that Jesus Son of Mary will descend, pursue and kill the Anti-Christ (Dajjāl), a figure who will appear on the world stage during the later times and cause much corruption and turmoil throughout the world.

[35] This is a reference to a Biblical nation that was completely destroyed by a fierce, scorching wind due to their mischief upon the Earth.

appear alongside the Anti-Christ." These authentic traditions and many more similar to them are well known and famous.

Around twenty-five years afterwards a revolution was stirred against the third caliph, ʿUthmān bin ʿAffān, by a hypocrite called **ʿAbdullāh bin Sabaʾ**. He spread ideological opposition towards ʿUthmān and mobilized the disgruntled riff-raff from various cities in Egypt and Irāq. They claimed he was hoarding wealth, creating class separation **and not judging with justice through God's law but by personal interests**. They descended upon the city of Medina during a time in which most of the Prophet's companions had gone for Ḥajj (pilgrimage) in Mecca. Around two-thousand in number, they surrounded ʿUthmān's house and besieged him for weeks. The Prophet's companions tried to intervene and resolve the situation, but ʿUthmān prohibited them as he did not want to be the cause of spilling any blood. Such was his concern for life, despite his full awareness that he was most likely to be murdered. Eventually, they broke into his house, stabbed the 80-year-old frail man repeatedly to death, looted all of his possessions and proceeded to raid the state treasury. This fulfilled the prophecy made by Muḥammad (peace be upon him) about the killing of ʿUthmān.

In the immediate aftermath of this assassination this renegade, insurgent group concealed itself amongst the local population in Medina. Whilst the Prophet's companions attempted to resolve this situation, differences of opinion appeared between them. There was no disagreement as to the validity of the leadership of ʿAlī who became the fourth caliph. Rather, the issue of contention was vengeance and justice for ʿUthmān. Taking the opportunity, the criminals managed to create civil strife first between ʿAlī and ʿĀʾishah (the Prophet's wife) and those with her such as Ṭalḥah and az-Zubayr who sought vengeance for ʿUthmān. And second, between the relatives of ʿUthmān such as Muʿāwiyah who were still pursuing justice for ʿUthmān and ʿAlī who still wanted to establish political authority and stability as an immediate crucial measure before pursuing the criminals. Some of the perpetrators and a large number of their followers remained in Medina whilst others had fled to Baṣrah in Irāq and other places. Their identities had not become clear and this exacerbated the problems between the parties.

The insurgents that remained in Medina eventually concealed themselves within Ali's army and managed to engineer two civil wars as a means of weakening the ability and resolve of the Prophet's companions to unite, pursue the criminals and bring them to justice. During the armed conflict which took place in 657 CE between ʿAlī and Muʿāwiyah, a call was made for an arbitration to end the hostilities just as ʿAlī's army was about to seal victory. Each side sent a representative to discuss the matter.

No sooner had agreement been reached to settle the matter through an arbitration at a later date that the leaders of the renegade insurgent group concealed within ʿAli's army began to stir up controversy. They began to claim that ʿAlī had **not judged by God's law**. They accused him of usurping God's authority and granting men the right to judge. They were also grieved that ʿAlī had not taken war booty, an indication that wealth was a motivating factor in their stance. As ʿAlī made his way back to Kufah, a large group of around 6,000 (and it is also said 12,000) deserted him and began to chant, "**Judgement is for none but God**." On the basis of this slogan, they excommunicated ʿAlī and the Prophet's companions on both sides of the conflict. They claimed ʿAlī and Muʿāwiyah had granted God's right to judge to men and the rest had become pleased with this act. This revealed their ignorance of basic Islāmic teachings, since God himself commands arbitration in disputes between contending parties in the Qurʾān and permits men to judge in those issues.

The renegades camped at a place called Ḥarūrāʾ not far from Kūfah. ʿAlī sent the cousin of the Prophet and most-learned scholar of the Qurʾān, Ibn ʿAbbās (d. 687), to debate them and remove their misconceptions and misunderstanding of basic Islāmic principles. When Ibn ʿAbbās went to them he noted that there was not a single companion of the Prophet amongst them. He proceeded to refute their three major misconceptions with his expert knowledge of the Qurʾān. A third of them recanted from their view. The others persisted on ascribing disbelief to ʿAlī and the Prophet's companions and continued in their seditious activities. These events fulfilled the prophecy made by Muḥammad (peace be upon him) that a renegade group would appear at a time when the Muslims would split into two groups.

The famous commentator of the Qurʾān and historian, **Ibn Kathīr** (d. 1373), recounts how the leaders of the Khārijite extremists met privately in the city of Kūfah intending to set up their Islāmic State in opposition to ʿAlī, who was the son-in-law and cousin of the Prophet.[36]

---

[36] Refer to "al-Bidāyah wal-Nihāyah" (10/578) onwards.

The renegades met in the house of **'Abdullāh bin Wahb al-Rāsibī** who admonished them, encouraged with abstinence from the world and to enjoin the good and prohibit the evil. He ordered the Khārijites to abandon the city of Kūfah because of its unjust laws, depart to the outskirts and mountains and start taking control of cities and townships. Then another one called **Ḥurqūṣ bin Zuhayr** stood and encouraged the others to seek truth and reject injustice. Another, **Sinān bin Ḥamzah**, stood and said that a leadership was needed in order to organise their affairs and for a flag to be raised to make their call open and known. They offered leadership to various individuals amongst themselves until it was accepted by ʿAbdullāh bin Wahb al-Rāsibī.

Later, they met in the house of **Zayd bin Ḥuṣayn al-Ṭāʾī**, a man who had previously threatened to kill ʿAlī in the same way they had previously killed ʿUthmān. In this gathering, he outlined their course of action. He recited the verse from the Qurʾān: **"Those who do not judge by what God has revealed, they are the disbelievers"** (5:44) and then said: "I testify against those who are intended by our call from the people who turn to Mecca in prayer that they have followed their desires and have thrown away the Book (of God). They have transgressed in speech and action (thereby leaving Islām) and waging jihād against them is a duty upon the Believers." Then another Khārijite stood up by the name of **'Abdullāh bin Shajarah** and began to entice the rest of them to attack the Muslims, saying: "Strike them on their faces and their foreheads with swords until the Most Gracious is obeyed (once more)."

After recounting these deeds of the very first Khārijites, Ibn Kathīr said almost seven centuries ago: "If these [Khārijites] were to acquire strength, they would corrupt the entire earth in Irāq and Syria and they would not leave a male or female child nor a man or woman (alive). This is because in their view the people (Muslims) have become corrupt in a way that nothing will rectify their situation except mass murder."[37]

Unwarranted excommunication (**Takfīr**) of Muslim rulers and their subjects based on dubious grounds and a twisted understanding of **Jihād** comprised the foundations of the Khārijite ideology. Upon their

---

[37] "Al-Bidāyah wal-Nihāyah" (10/585).

ignorance and extremism in these affairs they justified mass slaughter. These are the same ideas and activities inherited by al-Qaeda and ISIS as we shall outline further below.

The Khārijites continued to cause disturbances and rouse people against the leadership of ʿAlī, who showed gracious patience towards them. It was not until they slaughtered ʿAbdullāh bin Khabbāb, another companion of the Prophet, his household which included a pregnant woman and the emissary that ʿAlī later sent to verify the murder that he became resolved to fight them. He had recognized they were the group prophesized by Muḥammad (peace be upon him) over 25 years earlier and felt privileged that he should be the one to fight them.

By this time, the Khārijites had moved to a place called Nahrawān, twelve miles from Baghdād in Irāq and set up their own alleged **Islāmic State** as a means of countering the actual Islāmic State led by the Prophet's companions. From there, over a period of two years, they began to recruit people to join them from the various townships in Irāq and beyond. They attracted the young and ignorant and encouraged them to leave their parents, homes and townships because they had allegedly fallen into apostasy. In their view, emigrating to their alleged "Islāmic State" had become obligatory and a criterion of one's faith. In 659 CE, ʿAlī fought and defeated them at Nahrawān, fulfilling another prophecy of Muḥammad (peace be upon him). The survivors fled and dispersed to various lands and the seeds of this ideology remained. Filled with resentment and anger after their defeat, the Khārijites conspired to kill the main leaders of the Muslim nation. ʿAlī was the overall leader of the actual Islāmic state of the Muslims. Muʿāwiyah was the deputy leader in Syria and ʿAmr bin al-ʿĀṣ was the deputy leader in Egypt. Three men from the insurgent group conspired to assassinate all three leaders. Only the assassination of ʿAlī by a man named **Bin Muljam** was successful. He killed ʿAlī with a sword coated in poison whilst Alī was performing the dawn prayer in the grand mosque in Kūfah. The attempts on Muʿāwiyah in Syria and ʿAmr in Egypt failed.

The Khārijites continued in their subversive activities against the ruling authorities and they also developed their school of doctrine which was founded upon excommunication (takfīr) of the rulers upon the claim that they are unjust, hoard wealth which belongs to the masses and do not judge fully by God's law. By the end of the reign of the **Umayyads**, the first ruling dynasty, which lasted just over ninety years after the Khārijites appeared, at least eighteen revolutions were made against them, leading to turmoil, chaos and large numbers of

Muslims being killed. These revolutions continued during the reign of the **Abbasids** over the next 500 years and subsequently against other rulers in various lands. The Khārijites would appear whenever the seeds of this ideology were found along with the right set of circumstances. The Khārijites have never ceased to come out against the Muslims and their lands to this day. This is fulfilment of another prophecy of Muḥammad (peace be upon him) regarding their recurring appearance throughout the ages. From the above, it is important to note the following points which will help the reader in grasping the true reality of al-Qaeda and ISIS whose discussion is yet to follow:

First: The leaders of this **renegade terrorist group** were motivated by worldly matters pertaining to wealth. They were grieved by not receiving charity from the Prophet and challenged his integrity, claiming in effect that he did not judge by God's law but by personal interests. They resented ʿUthmān, the third caliph, because they were not given positions of power and were not receiving wealth they claimed they had a right to. They accused ʿUthmān of hoarding wealth, committing social injustice, tyranny and abandoning Islām. They were grieved that ʿAlī, the fourth caliph, did not fight and collect war booty which they would have had a share in. They accused ʿAlī of not judging by God's law and accused him of leaving Islām. In each of these three scenarios in which their ideology reared its ugly head, it can be observed that matters of the world were motivating them and each time they used the allegation of not judging by God's law to attack the leaders of the Muslims. This is what led the famous Islāmic scholar of the Qurʾān, Ibn Kathīr to state: "For the first innovation to occur in Islām was the tribulation of the Khārijites and their (ideological) starting point was due to [a matter] of the world."[38] **Second:** Their famous and most-distinguishing sign is to raise the slogan, "**Judgement is for none but God**" and to excommunicate the rulers of the Muslims because they do not judge fully by God's law. **Third:** They abandoned the main body of Muslims and set up their own rival "Islāmic State." They considered it obligatory to remove the leaders of the Muslims whom they imputed with apostasy and began to recruit people for this cause, considering this to be a religious obligation and a validation of faith. **Fourth:** They began to finance their "Islāmic State" by demanding charities from

---

[38] "Tafsīr al-Qurʾān al-Aẓīm" (2/10).

Muslims, informing them that it was unlawful to give their obligatory charity to the "apostate" Muslim leaders because they usurp wealth and squander it unjustly.

The Khārijites went on to develop their ideology further as they encountered new circumstances in their war against Islām and the main body of the Muslims. Their ideas and principles have been extensively documented in the Islāmic history books which were written three centuries after their appearance and proliferation into numerous sects. By way of example:

⦿ Their claim that because the Muslim rulers had left Islām by not abiding by justice and not juding by God's law, the lands under their control became lands of disbelief. Hence, the Muslim lands were divided into two categories: The **land of Islām (dār Islām)** in which they, the Khārijites, held power and the **lands of disbelief (dār kufr) and war (dār ḥarb)**, which were all other lands inhabited by Muslims. ⦿ Built upon the above, they began to demand that Muslims **emigrate to them** and leave the lands of disbelief, otherwise they would take the same judgement as the rulers. ⦿ They made it unlawful to pray behind the imāms of the mosques governed by the rulers of the Muslims. Hence, they gradually **abandoned Muslim societies** and avoided having any interactions with them. ⦿ They actively encouraged the common people to **hate their rulers** and roused their sentiments against them as a means of fermenting revolt and taking power. ⦿ They accused **the scholars of the Muslims** to be complicit in the tyranny and injustice of the rulers and extended the judgement of disbelief to them as well. ⦿ They would also interrogate people about their views on the Muslim rulers. Anyone who did not agree with their excommunication of the Muslim rulers would be judged an apostate and killed. ⦿ They permitted **the slaughter of women and children** upon numerous lines of argument including: They were married to or were the produce of apostates; they were collateral damage in the course of fighting apostates; their condition in terms of faith was unknown because they resided in a land of disbelief, hence killing them could not be considered blameworthy in the circumstances. ⦿ They permitted the killing of non-Muslims living under guarantee of protection. This was actually one of the cited reasons for ʿAlī fighting and killing them. ⦿ They described their activities in contending with the rulers and fighting against Muslims as "jihād" and "enjoining good" and "prohibiting evil" when in reality, it was nothing but corruption and evil. ⦿ To survive and maintain provisions they claimed it was lawful to **plunder and loot** the wealth of the tyrannical rulers and Muslims who did not openly subscribe to their ideology. ⦿ They permitted the use of **secrecy, violation of contracts** and clandestine operations such as **coups** and **assassinations**.

This group continued to appear and rise against the Muslims. Over the centuries, they plagued the major ruling dynasties, the Umayyads and the Abbasids. The famous historian and biographer, Imām al-Ẓahabī (d. 1348) mentions that due to the activities of certain Khārijite revolutionaries against the Umayyads and the Abbāsids, in excess of two and half million Muslims were slaughtered.[39] It should be clear to the reader from the above that this ideology is at war with Islām from its very foundations and that its primary target is in fact Islām, its rulers and its subjects. The Prophet said: "There will emerge a people from my nation from the East who recite the Qur'ān but it will not go beyond their throats. Every time a faction amongst them emerges it will be cut off. Every time a faction amongst them emerges it will be cut off", he repeated this ten times and then said: "Every time a faction amongst them emerges it will be cut off, until the Anti-Christ (Dajjāl) appears amongst their [later] remnants." He also said: "There will appear at the end of time a people who are young of age, foolish-minded. They will speak with the best [and most-alluring] of speech [that is spoken] by people and will recite the Qur'ān but it will not go beyond their throats. They will pass out of Islām as the arrow passes through its game. Whoever meets them, let him kill them, for there is a reward for whoever kills them."

As we proceed to discuss how this ideology appeared in the 20th century, one should keep in mind the two central tenets of this ideology: That the rulers have left Islām due to injustice and not ruling fully by God's law and that it is obligatory to wage "jihād" against them and against those who side with them. In short, they have extremism in **Takfīr** (excommunication) and an innovated, distorted concept of **Jihād** which is in reality, sedition, chaos, mischief, terrorism and destruction. In one phrase: **Takfīrī-Jihādist Khārijism**.

---

[39] "Siyar A'lām al-Nubulā'" (10/297).

9. What is the Islāmic position towards this group and its ideology?

The position of Islām towards the extremist, Khārijite renegades is so well known and famous that it is essentially an academic crime even to associate them with Islām in any form or fashion. When this group appeared, the Companions of the Prophet saw that numerous verses of the Qurʾān were revealed in relation to them them through God's foreknowledge. These verses include the saying of God: "**Say: Shall we inform you of the greatest losers as to [their] deeds? Those whose efforts have been wasted in this life while they thought that they were acquiring good by their deeds!**" (18:103-104).[40] Also: "**Some faces, that Day, will be humiliated. Labouring (hard in the worldly life), weary (in the Hereafter with humility and disgrace)**." (88:2-3).[41] And also: "**Those who break God's Covenant after ratifying it, and sever what God has ordered to be joined and do mischief on earth, it is they who are the losers**." (2:27).[42]

The traditions of the Prophet regarding them are abundant, well-known and famous. He prophesized their continued appearance throughout the ages and described them as "Dogs of Hellfire." He said of them: "They recite the Qurʾān but it does not pass their throats", "They are the most evil of creation", "They are the worst of those killed under the canopy of the sky", "If I was to reach them I would slaughter them like the slaughtering of ʿĀd."[43] He also ordered the leaders of his nation: "Kill them wherever you find them for there is a reward for the one who kills them." As for the Prophet's companions, then they implemented this legislative command and fought the Khārijites. ʿAlī, the Prophet's cousin and son-in-law was the first to wage war against them and defeat them at the headquarters of their alleged Islāmic state in Nahrawān, near the city of Baghdād, in 659 CE. And this remained

[40] Imām al-Ṭabarī mentions this application of the verse to the Khārijites and relates it from ʿAlī bin Abī Ṭālib.

[41] Imām al-Qurṭubī mentions this application of the verse to the Khārijites, citing it from ʿAlī bin Abī Ṭālib.

[42] Refer to "al-Iʿtiṣām" of al-Shāṭibī (1/90).

[43] This is a reference to a Biblical nation that was completely destroyed by a fierce scorching wind due to its iniquities. Muslim scholar, Ibn Ḥajar (d. 1449) explained this tradition to mean that if the Prophet had reached them, he would have wiped them out completely. Refer to Fatḥ al-Bārī (6/435).

the position of the scholars and leaders of the Righteous Predecessors (Salaf) over the next three hundred years. The Muslim scholars and jurists began to write about this group and its various sects, reviling them, abusing them, warning against them and refuting their misconceptions and their misguidance. Whilst the number of citations regarding them from 1300 years of Islāmic authorship can easily reach tens of thousands, we will suffice, for the sake of brevity, with just one concise statement from the notable Salafī scholar and jurist, **Abū Bakr Muḥammad al-Ājurrī** (d. 970) who mentioned the consensus of the Muslim scholars that the Khārijites are an evil, filthy, despicable people and that none of their apparent goodness is of any benefit to them. In his book titled "The Sharī'ah", he wrote the following: "The scholars have not differed that the Khārijite [extremists] are an evil people, disobedient to God and His Messenger, even if they pray, fast and strive hard in worship. None of that will be of benefit to them. They display the commanding of good and prohibiting of evil but that will not benefit them because they distort the Qur'ān with their desires and deceive the Muslims. God, the Most High, warned us against them. The Prophet warned us against them. The rightly-guided caliphs warned us against them. The Prophet's companions warned us against them. They are an evil, filthy despicable people. Those upon this doctrine continue to inherit it from each other [through the ages]. They revolt against the rulers and leaders and make lawful the killing of Muslims."[44] This position has been inherited throughout the centuries by Muslims adhering to the way of the Prophet and his companions.

10. How did this ideology appear in the 20th century?

The specific 20th century climate in which this ideology resurfaced starts with the dubious 19th century figure known as **Jamāl al-Dīn al-Afghānī** (d. 1897), an Iranian Shiite.[45] He travelled across the lands of

---

[44] "Al-Sharī'ah" (1/136).

[45] Al-Afghānī and his student, Muḥammad 'Abduh, are credited with creating the so-called "modern Salafist movement", but this is erroneous and is not a view shared by credible Orientalist scholars. These individuals made limited reference to the concept of "predecessors" to refer to an earlier fluid, dynamic, formative period in which deriving legal rulings from the texts (ijtihād) was being made to codify law. This was in contrast to the rigidity, stagnation

the Muslims (Egypt, Persia, Afghānistān, India, Turkey) creating political agitation. He is spuriously described as a "pan-Islāmist" and is alleged to have been working to revive the Islāmic empire. In actual reality, he was a revolutionary seeking to overturn the orderly state of affairs in the Muslim lands and alter their political and economic structures to facilitate outside influence and control. He promoted modernism and wanted a re-interpretation of Islām to fit with European ideals of progress and civilisation. In one of his works, al-Afghānī launched a Marxist, Communist diatribe against the third caliph ʿUthmān, accusing him of hoarding capital, nepotism, despotism and class separation. His most prominent student was **Muḥammad ʿAbduh** (d. 1905) who continued in the footsteps of his teacher and master.

A few decades later, using the same secretive organisational model of al-Afghānī and claiming the same alleged goals, the **Muslim Brotherhood** was founded in 1928 by **Ḥasan al-Bannā** (d. 1949) in Egypt. Its apparent aims were to resist colonialist influences and restore the Islāmic Caliphate. Al-Bannā was a staunch Ṣufī, however he would show different faces to different groups of people as a means of recruiting them into his organisation. This included unity and cooperation with Shiites. His brother, **ʿAbd al-Raḥmān al-Sāʿātī** was a staunch, fanatical Shiite. The Muslim Brotherhood therefore represented a combining of Ṣūfism and Shiism into a political force and an umbrella within which other orientations could be absorbed to increase its numbers. This "mass" could then be manipulated and mobilised to facilitate political goals through a variety of different routes whether voting in democracy or popular revolution. His party attempted to reach power through elections but during the 1940s acts of terrorism against the Egyptian society were committed by members of its "secret apparatus." This included throwing bombs in public places, the assassination of the judge Aḥmad Khazendar and the Prime Minister Maḥmūd al-Nuqrashi in 1948. The Egyptian scholar in the science of Prophetic traditions, Aḥmad Shākir, immediately characterised those

---

and blind-following that settled in amongst Muslims in the later period. These references were part of their wider goal of moving Muslim masses towards Modernism and imitation of Europe. They were not in any way referring to Salafism which is a call to pure Islām upon the way of the Prophet and his companions and the early generations of Muslims in creed, invitation (da'wah) and methodology.

behind these acts as Khārijites and described their pre-planned, politically motivated assassinations as acts of apostasy.[46]

During the same decade, the Indo-Pak writer and activist of Ṣūfī background, **Abū A'lā Mawdūdī** (d. 1979), began to devise a political ideology in which the greatest foundation of Islām was claimed to be leadership (imāmah), Shiism's most fundamental concept. It is important to note that Mawdūdī spoke ill of 'Uthmān, the third caliph and also reviled Mu'āwiyah, indicating that he was concealing the ideology of Shiism. He claimed that the most exclusive aspect of divinity was the right to issue laws. Because all Muslim rulers had usurped this right in his view, Mawdūdī encouraged the instigation of revolutions for their removal. To support this idea, he distorted the message and call of the prophets of God as detailed in the Qur'ān and claimed that their primary aim was to snatch political power and gain authority. Before his death in 1979, Mawdūdī praised **al-Khomeinī's Shiite revolution** in Irān as a genuine Islāmic revolution that demands the support of all Islāmic groups and parties working in the field of political activism. Mawdūdī was the first person to coin the term "hākimiyyah", representing God's unique and sole right to judge and paved the way for others to develop it further.

The Egyptian writer, **Sayyid Quṭb** (d. 1966), became the most influential figure in the revival of this Takfīrī-Jihādī ideology in the 20th century. He has an extremely colourful history.

Born in to a Ṣūfī family in 1906 in the Asyūt district of Egypt, he was nurtured upon the tradition of attachment and devotion to saints. As a youth he indulged in astrology and magic and would be solicited by young women to perform spells mostly for relationships. After graduating in Cairo in 1924 he worked as a teacher and editor and entered into the phase of materialist philosophies, doubt and atheism. During the 1930s Quṭb wrote in numerous newspaper columns and on

---

[46] In his article, "Faith prevents assassinations" published on 2nd January 1949 in the magazine, al-Asās. Aḥmad Shākir distinguished between acts of murder performed on a whim, such as what occurs during theft and the likes and politically-motivated, organised assassination of a Muslim ruler or figure of authority. The latter involves declaring deliberate murder to be lawful (istiḥlāl) which is disbelief, because it involves making lawful what God clearly declared unlawful . This is also the basis upon which Muslim scholars such as 'Abd al-'Azīz bin Bāz consider the Khārijites to be unbelievers and not Muslims.

one occasion he made a call for open nudity in the streets of Cairo. He became a literary critic, poet and writer over the next decade. Helmy Namnam, an Egyptian journalist who authored a book on the 1952 Socialist revolution in which Quṭb is said to have played a role, writes in this book that right up to 1948, Quṭb used to visit bars every now and then for a sip of cognac.

During the second world war, Quṭb used to write as Chief Editor for the official mouthpiece of the Grand Egyptian Freemasonic Lodge, titled "The Egyptian Crown". Within this paper he vehemently supported the Allied Forces and described the American and British as wagers of jihād (mujāḥidīn), messengers of democracy (rusul al-dīmuqrāṭiyah), men of truth (rijāl al-ḥaqq), our allies (ḥulafā'unā), our brothers (ikhwānunā), and he made supplication for them, saying, "God be with you" (Allāhu maʿakum).

In 1948, Qutb visited America for an unusually long period of two years. On his return he began to write on the subject of Islām with themes of social justice and began to interpret early Islāmic history through a Marxist, Socialist perspective. As a result, he attacked the third caliph ʿUthmān, described the revolution against him as one motivated by the "true Islāmic spirit" and also expelled Muʿāwiyah, his parents and his tribe, the Banī Umayyah, from Islām. Once more, we see the ideology of Shiism rearing its head through the writings and ideas of these thinkers.

In 1953, Quṭb entered the Muslim Brotherhood and shortly after fell into conflict with the Egyptian President, Jamāl ʿAbd al-Nāsser. During the 13 years till his death by hanging in 1966, Quṭb took the concept of Mawdūdī and developed it into a fully-fledged practical methodology: Mass excommunication, **Takfīr**, of all Muslim societies and calls for worldwide revolutions against them in the name of **Jihād**. This methodology was expounded within his Qur'ān commentary, "In the Shade of the Qur'ān" (Fī Ẓilāl al-Qur'ān) which he wrote based upon his opinions without reliance upon the Prophetic traditions. Whilst in prison, Quṭb encouraged his students to study the writings of Mawdūdī. He claimed that all contemporary Muslim societies had reverted to pre-Islāmic disbelief and barbarism (**jāhiliyyah**) because their rulers had usurped the right of God in rulership (**ḥākimiyyah**). He claimed their subjects had become satisfied with or indifferent to them and as such became their slaves and worshippers. A genuine Muslim society was non-existent and therefore Islām had been absent for many long centuries. In order to establish Islām again, revolution and war framed as "jihād" had to be launched against these "barbaric", "apostate" societies. Quṭb was strongly influenced by European revolutionary ideology as well as the writings of Mawdūdī. This ideology has much in common with the Marxist, Socialist revolutionary movements of the 19th and early 20th centuries and little to do with Islām. Rather, it clashes fundamentally with Islām and its ideals. Extracts from his Qurʿān commentary were separately published in a Leninist-style tract called "Milestones" (Maʿālim Fīl-Ṭarīq) and this became the manifesto for the 20th century Takfīrī-Jihādī ideology.

Meanwhile in Palestine, **Taqī al-Dīn al-Nabhānī** (d. 1977) a former Communist Baʿthist and nationalist revolutionary, set up the organisation known as **Ḥizb al-Taḥrīr** in 1953.[47] His ideas were the same as those of Mawdūdī and Quṭb: all contemporary rulers in Muslim lands are illegitimate, the lands ruled by them and inhabited by Muslims are lands of disbelief (dār kufr), the total absence of a genuine Muslim society and establishing the Caliphate being an individual obligation upon every Muslim. One can see a common theme amongst all of these writers in that they evaluated early Islāmic history through Marxist, Socialist, Communist spectacles and made claims similar to those bandits who revolted against ʿUthmān, ʿAlī and Muʿāwiyah, who

---

[47] Taqī al-Dīn al-Nabhānī has doctrinal roots that lie in the Ṣūfī Ashʿarī tradition along with Muʿtazilī influences. In the late 1940s he was involved in Baʿthist Communist and Nationalist movements. He was sent by ʿAbdullah al-Ṭall to Ḥusnī Zaʿīm in Damascus in 1949 to help engineer a revolution in Jordan after a successful coup had taken place in Syria in April of the same year, indicating that he was already involved in clandestine, revolutionary activities. Al-Nabhānī set up the organisation of Ḥizb al-Taḥrīr in 1953, modelling it on the secretive Baʿthist parties which he was involved in during the late 1940s. The structure of Ḥizb al-Taḥrīr as an organisation is based directly on the Communist "cell". They operate as a tight, rigid party with indoctrination upon the works of al-Nabhānī. Their entire approach is identical to Communist revolutionism. Al-Nabhānī simply "Islamicised" the Communist mode of operandum in the same way that Sayyid Quṭb clothed Leninism in Islāmic garb. One should note that individuals such as Mawdūdī, al-Nabhānī (and al-Khomeinī of Irān) authored works on "al-Ḥukūmah al-Islāmiyyah" (the Islāmic Government) centred around the doctrines of the Khārijites (ḥākimiyyah, implementing God's law) and the Shiites (imāmah, establishing leadership). These two sects wage war against Islām with their extremist ideologies.

were from the greatest of the companions of the Prophet (peace be upon him). The activities of those revolutionaries led to the emergence of the Khārijite and Shiite sects. The ideas of those sects were reproduced in the writings of these modern thinkers (al-Bannā, Mawdūdī, Quṭb and al-Nabhānī), and are thus, the true and real sources of extremist ideology in the 20th and 21st centuries.

The ideology that was born on account of these misguided men can again be summarised as a distortion of two familiar words: **Takfīr** and **Jihād**. The first represents excommunication of all contemporary Muslim rulers (and their subjects) on the basis of a distorted, political interpretation of Islām. The second is a reframing and distortion of jihād in Islām, an otherwise noble and lofty institution, into a struggle against "apostate" Muslim societies. This ideology is identical to that of the very first Khārijites who accused the Prophet's companions of not judging with justice in material affairs, excommunicated them, declared them to be apostates and revolted against them under the guise of "obligatory Jihād" in order to establish what was according to them the alleged "non-existent" Caliphate.

11. How did this ideology lead to the emergence of al-Qaeda?

Quṭb was hanged in 1966 and the Takfīrī-Jihādī Khārijite ideology which he developed and taught his followers in the prisons of Egypt led to the formation of two prominent extremist groups. During the 1970s, these two groups – **Jamā'ah Islāmiyyah** and **Jamā'at al-Jihād** – turned his writings into a fully independent school of thought and embarked upon spreading the Quṭbo-Mawdūdīan view of the world. They put the doctrines of Sayyid Quṭb into practice by calling for segregation and separation from the "apostate" Egyptian society and engaging in an organised struggle against the regime with acts of sedition and terrorism. Their activities culminated in the assassination of the Egyptian Prime Minister Anwar Sadat in 1981. Due to the Egyptian government clamping down on these extremists from the late 1960s onwards, some of these Takfīrī elements fled to the Gulf countries where they took up positions of teaching. They made use of their privileged positions to promote this extremist ideology in these new lands and began to create a **clandestine Muslim Brotherhood apparatus** within countries such as Saudi Arabia and the Emirates. The authorities of these countries had no reason at the time to suspect their activities and were unaware of their long-term agendas. This allowed them to spread their tentacles and poison the minds of a couple of generations who were nurtured with an innovated, heretical understanding of Islām. Additionally, in the 1980s, the Takfīrī elements from Egypt found another location to escape to: Afghānistān, to fight jihād against the Communist Soviets. The virus of Takfīrī ideology found fertile ground amongst many of the participants in this war and led to a merger between Jihād and Takfīrī ideology.

This inevitably brings us to **Osama bin Lādin**. Bin Lādin came from a Yemenī Ṣūfī family which had migrated to Saudi Arabia and entered the construction business. During the 1970s, he was nurtured upon the books and ideas of Sayyid Quṭb and Abu Aʿlā Mawdūdī.[48] He was a student of Sayyid Quṭb's brother, **Moḥammad Quṭb** (d. 2014), an Ashʿarī, and **ʿAbdullāh Azzām**, (d. 1989), a staunch follower of the doctrines of Sayyid Quṭb, member of the Muslim Brotherhood, well-known figure in the Afghānī Jihād and former student of Syrian Ṣūfīs Saʾīd Ḥawā and Muḥammad Saʾīd Ramadān al-Būṭī. After receiving his nurturing from the Muslim Brotherhood apparatus within Saudi Arabia, Bin Lādin went to Afghanistan to support the Jihād through his wealth and recruitment activities. In Afghanistan, the Takfīrī elements who arrived from Egypt began to spread their ideology through writings and publications. They distributed the works of Quṭb and Mawdūdī and also started authoring their own books centered around the excommunication of Muslim rulers in the Gulf countries and outlining

---

[48] Muṣtafā Wafā, General Trustee of the Council for Islāmic Research for the Commitee of Major Scholars of al-Azhar (Egypt) is cited as saying, "The words used by **Bin Lādin** in his speech confirms that he is affected a great deal by the books of **Sayyid Quṭb** and the deceased **Abū Aʿlā Mawdūdī**. He conveys the thoughts of Sayyid Quṭb in his book, 'Milestones', in which he divided the world into Muslim, disbeliever and sinner, or into the faithful society and the society of (pre-Islāmic) ignorance. Bin Lāden tried to to differ from the group of the Muslim Brotherhood (al-Ikhwān) by bringing out the ideology of Sayyid Quṭb in a practical way. Just as he also studied well the books of Abū Aʿlā Mawdūdī, especially 'al-Muṣṭalaḥāṭ al-Arbaʾ'. And these books specifically were the primary, chief movers behind the Islāmic activism of the youth of the various Islāmic parties in the 1970s during the previous century. And I think that Bin Lādin was amongst those who was politicised (into activism) during this era." As cited on Sahab.Net and numerous other sources from a report titled, "Figureheads and Indications in the Speech of Bin Lādin."

the alleged "forgotten obligation" of waging jihād against them. Another important figure to appear in this period was **Ayman al-Zawāhirī**, an Egyptian who was amongst those imprisoned in Egypt, a disciple of Quṭb's teachings and a staunch Takfīrī Khārijite. He, along with those previously mentioned, influenced Bin Lādin. When those affected by this ideology returned to their countries from the Afghānī Jihād, they saw their societies in a new way: Apostates who had revoked Islām and needed to be invited to Islām afresh. This is why one Saudi scholar said: "They left for Afghānistān considering us Muslims and returned considering us infidels." It must be emphasised here that this extremist political ideology does not have its basis in "Wahhābī" or Salafī interpretations of Islām, despite claims to the contrary.[49] Rather, the original figureheads of this ideology in the 20th century come from the Ṣūfī, Ashʿarī schools of thought who combined European revolutionary ideologies with the poison of the Khārijites and the poison of the revolutionary Shiites.

During the 1980s, books written by the leaders of this extremist ideology such as **Abū Muḥammad al-Maqdisī**[50] and the Egyptian Jihādi ideologist and Muftī for al-Qaeda, **ʿAbd al-Qādir ʿAbd al-ʿAzīz (Sayyid Faḍl)**, included gross distortions and misinterpretations of the writings of prominent figures such as Ibn Taymiyyah and Muḥāmmad bin ʿAbd al-Wahhāb. Western academics and scholars of Islām have failed to accurately and truthfully characterise these extremist bandits as Khārijites. Instead, they began to ascribe the roots of this ideology to "Wahhābism" or Salafism. The political ideology of Abū Aʿlā Mawdudī and Sayyid Quṭb which paved the way for 20th century **Khārijite Takfīrī-Jihādism** cannot be found in the books of these two scholars, Ibn Taymiyyah or Muḥammad Ibn ʿAbd al-Wahhāb. In fact, the various elements of this ideology are extensively refuted in the writings of both of these scholars and their students.

The Takfīrī-Jihādī ideology became a destructive, seditious enterprise to wage war against Muslim societies and overturn

---

[49] The Takfīrī Jihādists consider the rulers and scholars of Saudi Arabia in particular and the Gulf countries in general to be their greatest enemies. They never studied directly with the scholars from these countries but were nurtured upon the revolutionary ideologies of Quṭb and Mawdūdī.

[50] In some of his writings, Abū Muḥammad al-Maqdisī, a key ideologist of Takfīrī-Jihādism, acknowledges that his primary nurturing in Islāmic teachings was based upon the writings of Sayyid Quṭb and Abū Aʿlā Mawdūdī.

governments. Many new concepts appeared during the 80s and 90s in their writings. From them: The concept of the "near enemy" and the "distant enemy". Muslim societies in the form of rulers, government institutions, the police, the military, imāms, scholars and the general public who did not join them were considered the greater "**near enemy**" who had to be fought first. The "distant enemies" were non-Muslim nations and their subjects. Also, the doctrine: "Whoever does not excommunicate a disbeliever (meaning a Muslim who is accused of apostasy by the Takfīrī Khārijites) is himself a disbeliever" was used to expand the charge of disbelief against opponents. Likewise, they used the doctrine of loyalty and disloyalty as a weapon to expand the judgement of disbelief to all of their opponents and detractors. These were symptoms of the Takfīrī-Jihādī virus and its destructive effects soon followed.

For example, in Algeria, the adoption and spread of this doctrine amongst insurgents and revolutionaries led to the death of over 100,000 Muslims. Whole towns of innocent men, women and children were often massacred brutally. Similarly, Khārijite terrorists attacked oil facilities in Saudi Arabia in the 1990s, and this was followed by a string of bombings that have not ceased till today. This signalled the appearance of **al-Qaeda** on the world scene in the 1990s with the original intent of putting the methodology of Sayyid Quṭb and Abū Aʿlā Mawdūdī into solid practice. Its primary focus was on Muslim rulers, particularly those of the Gulf, whom they had excommunicated from Islām. They considered the rulers of these lands to be the greatest enemies of Islām and most worthy of removing through jihād.

As for their position towards non-Muslims and their governments, the Khārijites were not really interested in them and had such governments not meddled in the affairs of Muslim countries for their own agendas and goals, al-Qaeda would have continued to progress their Khārijite agenda in the Muslim lands through sedition and terrorism.[51] These insurgents were grieved that foreign meddling in

---

[51] It must be noted that Western governments have routinely found utility in Takfīrī-Jihādī Khārijite movements. They were actively supported during the Afghan war in the 1980s when Osama bin Lādin was hailed a hero. This support was led by Zbigniew Brzezinski, security advisor to President Jimmy Carter, with involvement of Western intelligence agencies. In the 1990s, the same Jihādī elements were given tactical support against Serbia, a Christian

these lands has come in the way of their own agenda which is waging jihād against the Muslim rulers, governments and subjects.

Over time however, the tactic of the Khārijites has somewhat changed, at least in some quarters. Some of the themes developed in their recent writings over the past decade include plans to deliberately entice foreign forces into the lands of the Muslims as a means of triggering a large scale war in which they believe they will be victorious over "apostate" Muslim societies and foreign invaders.

For the Neoconservatives[52] and their agendas, this could not be greater news. Muslim scholars throughout the centuries have made note of the destructive nature of this movement. **Imām al-Ṭabarī** (d. 923) said: "The Khārijites would meet each other and remember the location (of battle) of their brothers [of old] at al-Nahrawān (the place of their first breakaway Islāmic State which was defeated by ʿAlī). They held that remaining idle amounted to cheating and weakness and that in [the activity of] making jihād against the Muslims (ahl al-qiblah) lay excellence and reward."[53] **Ibn Ḥazm al-Andalūsī** (d. 1064) said: "And

---

ally of Russia. More recently, the same Takfīrī-Jihādī elements were given support against Muʿammar al-Ghaddāfī, leading to his demise and the descent of Libya into turmoil and chaos. Likewise, in Syria, "moderate rebels" (al-Qaeda Jihādists) were actively encouraged and supported financially and militarily to help in the removal of Bashar al-Assad. The astute observer will note that these Khārijites have aided Western governments tremendously in both their domestic (security) and foreign policies by facilitating the "long war": The means through which the central-Asian basin, the richest and most strategically important land mass on Earth, can be partitioned and reshaped to enable development, control and exploitation of its vast natural resources.

[52] Neoconservatives ("Neocons" for short) follow a political philosophy which advocates the use of aggressive force, manipulation and deception as a means of maintaining political and military supremacy and paving the way for large corporations to control and shape the politics and economies of other nations. Some of their key figures are William Kristol and Robert Kagan. They influence and shape government policies via think-tanks and tax-exempt foundations. In September 2000 they issued a report outlining their visions of a new century of conquest starting in central Asia. General Wesley Clark – Retired 4-star U.S. Army general, Supreme Allied Commander of NATO during the 1999 War on Yugoslavia – can be found on Youtube saying that in late 2001 he was personally informed of plans to "take out" Afghānistān, Irāq, Libya, Syria and several other countries over a period of 10 years.

[53] "Tārikh al-Ṭabarī" (5/174).

they do not cease to strive in overturning the orderly affairs of the Muslims (into chaos) and splitting the word of the believers. They draw the sword against the people of religion and strive upon the Earth as corrupters. As for the Khārijites and Shiites, their affair in this regard is more famous than that one should be burdened in mentioning."[54] **Ibn Taymiyyah** (d. 1328) said: "For they (the Khārijites) strived to kill every Muslim who did not agree with their view, declaring the blood of the Muslims, their wealth, and the slaying of their children to be lawful, whilst excommunicating them. They considered this to be worship, due to their ignorance and their innovation which caused [them] to stray."[55] Both Muslim scholars and non-Muslim academics have pointed out the strong resemblance between the Khārijites and the Marxist, Communist revolutionary movements. They accuse the rulers of misuse of state capital, class separation, nepotism, tyranny and not establishing social justice. They then revolt, mobilise the masses if they are able, and overturn the orderly state of affairs. Once they have taken power, the leaders and instigators at the top begin their mass slaughter of the masses and anyone whom they believe might be able to launch a counter-revolution. This ideology is simply a tool for acquiring wealth (māl) and authority (wilāyah) and eliminating all opposition once the objective has been attained. The Khārijites share with the Marxists and Communists in their deceptive cloaks of "social justice" and "equal distribution of wealth" and have simply added the cloak of religion as a means of recruiting foot soldiers.

12. How did al-Qaeda transform into ISIS?

Following the events of 11 September 2001[56] and the pre-planned illegal, imperial invasions of Afghānistān and Irāq, Jihādists led by **Abū**

---

[54] "Al-Faṣl Fī al-Milal al-Ahwā' wal-Niḥal" (5/98).

[55] "Minhāj al-Sunnah" (5/248).

[56] Many high ranking figures in politics and intelligence state firmly that 9/11 was not executed by radical extremists led by Osama bin Lādin from a cave in Afghānistān. They include Francesco Cossiga, the former President and Prime Minister of Italy (1985-1992), Andreas von Bulow, former German Defense Minister and Alan Sabrosky, former Director of Studies at the U.S. Army War College–Strategic Studies Institute. They are amongst an ever-growing number of thousands of politicians, analysts and highly-ranking specialists in the fields

Musab al-Zarqāwī (d. 2006) who had fought in Afghanistan formed an alliance with Osama bin Lādin and created "al-Qaeda in Irāq." They fought against the Shiite Irāqī government that had been installed as well as the American occupation. Their activities included attacking innocent Sunnī Muslims who did not agree with their ideology and they would bomb markets and mosques alike. Al-Zarqāwī was killed in 2006 and later in the year, "**The Islāmic State of Irāq**" (al-Dawlah al-Islāmiyyah Fīl-ʿIrāq) was announced. Its leader was Abū ʿUmar al-Baghdādī (d. 2010). This group attempted to unite various Jihādī factions operating in Irāq. After Abū ʿUmar al-Baghdādī was killed, **Abu Bakr al-Baghdādī** became its leader. Indiscriminate bombings in streets, markets and mosques in Baghdād and elsewhere were performed by this group based upon its extremist Takfīrī ideology and much of their fighting was against rival groups who had not come under their authority.

Meanwhile, the **2011 Syrian Revolution** led to the mobilisation of al-Qaeda elements from places such as Libya, Tunisia and Egypt. Given open passage to Syria, they were subsequently provided with tactical support by Western governments because toppling Bashār al-Assad is a primary regional geopolitical objective. **The Nuṣrah Front** (Jabhah al-Nuṣrah) was one of the main opposition forces and they were under the direction of Ayman al-Zawāhirī as representatives of al-Qaeda in Syria. They, along with other anti-Syrian government factions were loosely referred to as "moderate rebels". Over the next few years, this stoking of conflict and revolution in Syria led to chaos, turmoil and much spilling of blood.

---

of intelligence, structural engineering, aviation and controlled demolition who share this view. Numerous Muslim scholars express the view that not all alleged terrorist attacks are perpetrated by radical Muslims. In instances, intelligence agencies of certain governments or Iranian Shiites pretending to be Sunnī Muslims perpetrate attacks to implicate Sunnī Muslims to facilitate geopolitical objectives. At the same time, this does not mean that Khārijite extremists do not perpetrate acts of terrorism. However, the vast majority of their terrorism is against Muslims, not Westerners. These attacks are not reported in Western media with the same level of coverage as attacks in the West. This gives the false impression that the Khārijite terrorists only target Westerners and that they are at war with the West. In reality, they are at war with Islām and Muslims (the "near enemy") before they are at war with anyone else, and they explicitly state this in their writings.

Then in 2013, Abu Bakr al-Baghdādī announced the formation of **"The Islāmic State of Irāq and Syria"**, (al-Dawlah al-Islāmiyyah Fīl-ʿIrāq wal-Shām), or **ISIS** (Daesh) for short. A very large number of the Nuṣrah Front fighters in northern Syria reaching into many thousands immediately affiliated with this new organisation. The main spokesman of ISIS, Abū Muḥammad al-ʿAdnānī demanded that all Jihādī groups participating in the conflict join the ISIS project. Whilst this led to subsequent in-fighting between the Takfīrī-Jihādists which has not ceased till this day, the alleged "Islāmic State" came out as the largest group in the area and managed to take control of key regions and cities such as Raqqa in Syria and Moṣul in Irāq. These areas include oil producing regions. Over the past two years they have continued in their campaign of brutal killings and mass slaughter as a means of increasing their power and land base.

The alleged "Islāmic State" is rejected by all Muslim countries, rulers and scholars as unfounded and illegitimate. Their ideology is that of the first Khārijites thereby excluding them from having any legitimate authority. Prominent Muslim scholars such as Ibn Taymiyyah have classified the Khārijites as one of the primary targets of legitimate Islāmic jihād that is performed under the supervision of the rulers of the Muslims. The leaders of ISIS are no different to the leaders of the very first Khārijites whose mention has preceded such as ʿAbdullāh bin Wahb al-Rāsibī and Zayd bin Ḥuṣayn al-Ṭāʾī. ISIS consider all Muslim rulers to be apostates. They consider their lands to be lands of disbelief and war. They claim to have established an "Islāmic Caliphate" and require all Muslims to pledge allegiance to it, migrate to them and engage in "jihād" against the Muslim rulers or against competing factions who vie with them for wealth, land and authority.[57] Further, just like the very first Khārijites had methods of recruitment by which they enticed the young and foolish to abandon their families and homes to join them, ISIS also make use of slick, emotional propaganda. They use injustices against Muslims as cheap merchandise to call to their evil ideology, despite the fact that they themselves slaughter Muslims mercilessly and behave with them in the most horrendous of ways. Well-informed, knowledgeable Muslims who follow the guidance of the

---

[57] Fighting has been ongoing between rival Takfīrī-Jihādī groups such as ISIS and al-Nuṣrah and is a natural consequence of their destructive ideology.

orthodox Salafī scholars of Islām know that these are the very people whom the Prophet of Islām spoke about when he said: **"They recite the Qur'ān but it does not pass beyond their throats."**, **"They exit from Islām as swiftly as the arrow passes straight through its target."**, **"They are the worst of creation."**, **"They are the worst of those killed beneath the canopy of the sky."**, **"They are the Dogs of Hellfire."**, **"If I was to reach them, I would slaughter them, like the slaughtering of 'Ād."**[58], **"Kill them wherever you find them for there is a reward for the one who kills them."**

It should be clear from what has preceded that al-Qaeda, ISIS and any other group in any part of the world that shares their ideology are at war with Islām and its people. These theological and historical facts also expose those who display enmity towards Islām and try to ascribe the deeds of the Khārijites to Islām and its teachings. This is despite the Prophet's statements that the Khārijites depart from Islām, do not understand the Qur'ān, are the worst of creation, fight and kill Muslims and must be fought, killed and eliminated under the leadership of the Muslim rulers.

13. Does ISIS serve the interests of Muslims and their lands?

We have now established with evidences that al-Qaeda and ISIS are Khārijite renegades pure and clear. Their ideological foundations are identical to the first sect to break away from the main body of Muslims. The answer is therefore obvious in that they do not serve the interests of Muslims at all. Muslim scholars have considered heretical groups like the Khārijites to be like **trojan horses** whose harm to the Muslims is much greater than that of a warring enemy.[59] Further, many Muslim scholars past and present have explained that these subversive elements are often manipulated and directed from the outside to further foreign interests which are detrimental to the well-being of Muslims, their countries and their lands. In reality, ISIS is a tool.

---

[58] This is a reference to a Biblical nation that was completely destroyed by a fierce, scorching wind due to their mischief upon the Earth.

[59] Scholars such as Abū al-Wafā' Ibn 'Aqīl (d. 1119), Abd al-Ghanī al-Maqdisī (d. 1203) and Ibn Taymiyyah (d. 1328) have indicated this.

The Mufti of Saudi Arabia, ʿAbd al-ʿAzīz Āl al-Shaykh remarked last year: "The terrorism of ISIS is the very first enemy of Islām."[60] Recently, he stated that ISIS (Daesh) are simply fighters serving the region-wide interests of other nations and not those of Muslim countries.[61] In an interview given to the Ukkāẓ newspaper, he stated that ISIS are "a faction in whose hearts is a disease and evil intentions towards Islām and its people." He also stated: "The Islāmic military alliance set up by the Kingdom with the participation of thirty-five states is a beneficial alliance and a response to the mischief-makers in order to halt them at their limits." He stated: "Had it not been for God granting success in setting up this alliance (against the terrorists), these enemies would continue to occupy the lands of the Muslims." He also explained that these terrorists are directed to help fulfil frightening plans. The Muftī emphasized this by saying: "They have only come in order to point their weapons towards Muslims." He also said: "These Khārijite groups are not to be considered Islāmic nor to be amongst the people of Islām who hold fast to its guidance. Rather, they are an extension of the Khārijites who were the first sect to depart from the religion due to their excommunication of Muslims on account of mere sins and making lawful their blood and the seizing of their wealth."

Political commentators and analysts including Zionist Jews express the view that ISIS is good for Israel.[62] This is because the presence of ISIS and its subversive ideology in various Muslim countries is a destabilising force which keeps them weak and in disarray, both economically and politically, if not overturning them completely. Writing for the Israeli Haaretz newspaper, correspondent, Zvi Bar'el writes: "While Israel is pounding Gaza, it's good to know that at least one Muslim organisation isn't rushing to threaten Israel. This refreshing news comes from the organisation known until about a week or two ago as ISIS, but which now – since it has started to consolidate its hold on a stretch of territory linking Iraq and Syria – calls itself the Islāmic

---

[60] This was covered in many leading Arabic newspapers in August 2014. Refer to http://arabic.cnn.com/middleeast/2014/08/19/saudi-mufti-isis.

[61] In an article published on http://alarab.com on 28 December 2015.

[62] It must be made clear that not every Jew is a Zionist and not every Zionist is a Jew. Organisations such as "Neturei Karta" or "True Torah Jews" consider Zionism to be a secular political ideology clashing with orthodox Judaism and harmful to the interests of Jews worldwide (who are supposed to live in exile).

State... The Islāmic State's target bank contains a long list of Arab leaders – including the Saudi and Jordanian kings, the prime minister of Iraq, the president of Egypt and even the leadership of the Muslim Brotherhood – before it gets to the Jews and Israel."[63] In other words, by the time ISIS ever decides to make an invasion of Israel, all of Israel's neighbours will have been attacked, ravaged and practically eliminated as a threat to Israel if ISIS continues and has its way.

In his article for the Jerusalem Post on 8 September 2015 titled, "Analysis: How Dangerous is ISIS to Israel?", Professor of Political studies at Bar-Ilan University in Tel Aviv, Efraim Inbar writes: "It is misplaced to view ISIS as posing an independent serious strategic challenge [to Israel]." Further, many Jewish communities across Europe and America have deplored the attempts by Israeli Prime Minister Benjamin Netanyahu to capitalise on terrorist attacks linked to ISIS by urging them to move to Israel. By way of example, one can read the article, "European Jews Rebuff Netanyahu's Call to Migrate to Israel" published in the Wall Street Journal on 18 February 2015. This article is one of many which reveal that thousands of Jews who live happily in their host nations, and have done for generations or centuries, are discerning enough to see through hardline Zionist propaganda for which the terrorist activities in the West linked to ISIS are both very convenient and extremely useful.

It ought to be clear for any person, Muslim or non-Muslim, to see that the terrorism of al-Qaeda, ISIS and groups with a similar ideology such as Boko Ḥarām and al-Shabāb, does not serve the interests of Muslims, their lands, their economies or their political stability. These groups bring untold calamities upon Muslims who are their primary targets and greatest victims and they open up the doors to outside parties who take advantage of the situation to pursue their own economic and geopolitical agendas. They bring calamities due to their violation of one of the greatest foundations of Islām which has been strongly emphasized by orthodox scholars throughout the centuries such as Aḥmad bin Ḥanbal (d. 855), Ibn Taymiyyah (d. 1328) and Muḥammad Ibn ʿAbd al-Wahhāb (d. 1792). This great foundation is: To have patience upon the rulers despite their injustice and tyranny and not to bring about greater evil through sedition and revolt which lead to bloodshed, the removal of security, the destruction of livelihood and

---

[63] "Why the Islāmic State Isn't in Any Rush to Attack Israel", 15 July 2014.

welfare and granting opportunity to third-party interlopers to pursue their own agendas.

This principle was laid down by the Prophet for his nation as a means of protection for his nation. From his numerous, abundant, famous statements in this regard is when he said to one of his companions called Hudhayfah: "There will be after me rulers who do not guide themselves by my guidance nor follow my Sunnah and there will appear amongst you men whose hearts are the hearts of devils in the bodies of men." Hudhayfah asked: "What shall I do if I reach that [time]?" He said: "Hear and obey the ruler, even if your back is beaten and your wealth is confiscated."[64] The emphatic nature of this principle in Islām can be seen by the fact that whereas patience has been ordered towards the tyranny and injustice of the sinful rulers on the one hand, fighting and killing the Khārijites has been ordered on the other, despite their apparent display of piety and alluring, beautified claims of "removing tyranny", "establishing justice" and "establishing the Caliphate".

14. Is Western foreign policy the cause of this extremist ideology?

Western foreign policy in the Middle East and Central Asia is not the cause of the existence of these extremists or their ideology. It is an evil ideology **diametrically opposed** to everything Islām stands for and it appeared at the very dawn of Islām in a people motivated by other than Islām but acting upon the pretence that it is Islām. They waged war against the Prophet's companions and remain a tribulation upon the Muslims to this day.

Invoking foreign policy as the sole cause of extremism is used by terrorist sympathizers to justify or explain away the atrocities committed by these evil people. They downplay, if not conceal, the underlying evil, heretical Khārijite ideology which appeared as a war against Islām and its adherents. In effect, these misguided people are saying that the severe warnings of the Prophet Muḥammad (peace be upon him) against the Takfīrī Khārijite sect and its ideology can be ignored. It's allegedly not the fault of the extremists and terrorists for murdering

---

[64] Related by Muslim in his Ṣaḥīḥ.

civilians because Western governments forced them to into this ideology and these activities.

The same apologists also mention the lifestyles of Muslim rulers and the presence of social inequality in Muslim lands as an excuse for the Khārijite ideology, thereby also intending to say: "It's not their fault, the circumstances forced these beliefs upon them, how else should we expect them to react?" This is an evil narrative propounded by ignoramuses who do not value the basics of Islāmic theology. This argument is employed to excuse the extremists and to ignore, if not to help perpetuate the evil, misguided ideology underlying their corrupt activities. The Prophet anticipated these affairs of tyranny and injustice through revelation and gave guidance regarding them. These people do not value the Prophetic guidance and the judgements made therein regarding this extremist ideology and its adherents whose recurring appearance has been textually stated.

We have already noted that this ideology took shape in the first half of the 20th century through the writings of certain misguided thinkers and activists, well before the contemporary period of occupation and conflict in Muslim countries. Hence, its origins have nothing to do with current Western foreign policy. Had there not been a single American, British or European soldier in any Muslim country, the followers of the Khārijite ideology would still be committing bloodshed through their seditious activities. Indeed, they were already doing so long before the illegal, unjust invasions of Afghānistān and Irāq. The conflicts in these regions merely gave these groups the opportunity to congregate and organise and are not causes of their extremist ideology.

15. Do al-Qaeda and ISIS target only Westerners?

The primary targets of Khārijite Takfīrī Jihādists are Muslims. Research has established that the overwhelming majority of victims of this ideology are Muslims. This has always been the case throughout history and will always remain the case as it is stated explicitly in the Prophetic traditions. In a 2009 report by the **Combating Terrorism Center** based at the US Military Academy in West Point titled "Deadly Vanguards: A Study of al-Qaeda's Violence Against Muslims", the authors Scott Helfstein, Nāssir ʿAbdullāh and Muḥammad al-ʿObaidi established through a solid research methodology that al-Qaeda kills eight times more Muslims than non-Muslims, and even more when the division is expanded into Western and non-Western victims.

A 2015 report titled "**The New Jihadism**" which was published by the Department of War Studies at King's College London indicates that during the month of November 2014, chosen as a sample month for the study, a total of 664 attacks led to the deaths of 5042 people, the overwhelming majority of which were in Irāq (1770), Nigeria (786), Afghānistān (782), Syria (693), Yemen (410), Somalia (216) and Pakistan (212).[65] Peter Neumann, the author of the report states: "This report, therefore, tells the story of a movement in the middle of a transformation – one whose final outcome is impossible to predict. The immediate focus, however, is jihadism's human cost: with, on average, more than 20 attacks and nearly 170 deaths per day, jihadist groups destroy countless lives – most of them Muslim – in the name of an ideology that the vast majority of Muslims reject." And he notes in the conclusion: "In just one month, jihadist groups ḳilled 5,042 people – the equivalent of three attacks on the scale of the London bombings in July 2005 each day. Contrary to the often articulated complaint that jihadism is over-reported and that groups like the Islāmic State get too much coverage, our survey seems to suggest that most of the victims receive practically no attention. Hardly any of the attacks that formed the basis for our analysis were reported in the Western media. Indeed, even the suicide bombings – of which there were 38 – made virtually no headlines except in the countries in which they took place. Yet most of the victims of jihadist violence continue to be non-combatants, and the vast majority is Muslim."[66]

Karen Armstrong, a British author and commentator, known for her authoritative books on comparative religion and Islām, stated: "I think one of the things we should do is mourn their dead too. Not long ago 165 Pakistani children were shot by the Taliban. Two thousand villagers in Nigeria were slaughtered by Boko Haram. But we're not marching for them. So the impression we give is that we just don't care, that their lives are not so valuable to us. So I think we must take notice that we're not the only ones begin killed by extremists. **Far more Muslims are dying**."[67]

---

[65] "The New Jihadism: A Global Snapshot", Peter Neumann, International Centre for the Study of Radicalization, Kings College London. p. 14.

[66] "The New Jihadism", p. 23.

[67] Online interview with Dutch paper, Nieuwwij.nlo, 18 January 2015.

It is no longer disputed that Muslims are the greatest victims of terrorism perpetrated in the name of Islām. To well-informed Muslims, this is not news. This is because from the prominent traits of the Khārijites mentioned by the Prophet Muḥammad (peace be upon him) is that they kill the people of Islām and leave alone those besides them.[68] Terrorist incidents in the West that involve Muslims as perpetrators receive focused, sustained and emotive news coverage whereas those in which Muslims are the victims in various parts of the world do not receive the same attention, if any at all. This naturally creates the false, inaccurate perception that terrorism performed in the name of Islām is directed primarily and only towards non-Muslims and that Muslims are engaged in a war against the West.

This is very far from the truth as has preceded in our discussion of the Khārijite ideology. Unfortunately, this incorrect perception is the basis upon which right-wing groups further their own agendas. They blame Muslims and return everything to Islām, when Islām is free and innocent of the terrorists, just as Jesus (peace be upon him) is free and innocent of the **Ku Klux Klan**, the **IRA**, **Anders Breivik**, the **Tripura** and **Nagaland terrorists** (India), the **Phineas Priesthood** (USA), the barbaric **Anti-Balaka** terrorists (Central African Republic) and the barbaric **Lord's Resistance Army** (Uganda). This latter group of Christians – in the name of establishing Biblical law – have displaced millions of people, slaughtered at least 100,000 over 15 years by conservative estimates and kidnapped tens of thousands of children, using them as sex-slaves and soldiers. They have slaughtered more people than al-Qaeda and ISIS combined, yet we never see dramatic, sensational media coverage of their atrocities on prime-time television. The reason is obvious, it's because they are Christians.

---

[68] These traditions can be found in the collections of al-Bukhārī and Muslim. Terrorism in Western lands is merely a by-product, not something primarily intended by the Khārijites. Their primary targets are Muslim governments and their subjects. Imām al-Ājurrī (d. 970), said: "The scholars, past and present have not differed that the Khārijites are an evil people, disobedient to Allāh the Exalted and His Messenger (peace be upon him), even if they pray, fast and strive in worship. They claim to enjoin the good and prohibit the evil, but that will not benefit them... The Khārijites are evil, impure and vile, as are all the [variant] factions of Khārijites who are upon their doctrine. They revolt against the rulers and make lawful the killing of Muslims." In his excellent book titled, al-Sharī'ah (1/136).

16. Are Muslims obligated by Islām to establish a worldwide caliphate?

The claim that all Muslims are obligated by their faith to work towards establishing a worldwide caliphate is false and has no basis in any text in the Qurʾān or the Prophetic traditions. This is a modern political ideology which relies upon a distortion of the message of the prophets of God in general and of Prophet Muḥammad in particular. This idea began to surface in the speeches and writings of **Ḥasan al-Bannā** (d. 1949), founder of the Muslim Brotherhood in Egypt, **Abū Aʿlā Mawdūdī** (d. 1979), the Indo-Pak subcontinent writer and activist, **Sayyid Quṭb** (d. 1966) from Egypt who developed the core ideas laid down by Mawdudī and **Taqī al-Dīn al-Nabhānī** (d. 1977) who was the founder of Hizb al-Taḥrīr in the 1950s. These writers presented the idea that no true Muslim society exists today because Muslim rulers have usurped the authority of God by becoming lawgivers. As a result, the lands they rule over are lands of disbelief, not lands of Islām and they must therefore be removed. Jihād is then presented as the struggle against these rulers in order to establish a caliphate. This idea has never been known to Muslims prior to that except from the very first sect to break off from Islām, the Khārijites. Those responsible for this heresy such as Mawdūdī, Quṭb and al-Nabhānī were strongly influenced by Marxist, Leninist, Communist revolutionary ideology in their writings and the methodologies they proposed. Making leadership (imāmah, ḥukūmah) the first foundation of religion is a Shiite concept and demands a revolutionary mindset. This helps to explain why the above thinkers presented Shiite concepts in their writings to varying degrees and also had personal connections with prominent Shiites.

Muslims are obligated to worship God alone, establish the five pillars, fulfil the obligations and keep away from the prohibitions to the best of their ability. They have been ordered to follow the guidance of the Prophet (peace be upon him) and excel in morals and character. They have been ordered to behave as faithful subjects under the authority of the ruler whether he is pious or sinful. They have been prohibited from revolting against tyrannical rulers so as to prevent greater evil from engulfing the society at large. They have been ordered to abide by their covenants, agreements and contracts. Attempting to snatch power through political or violent means in order to establish authority is not permitted in Islām and leads to chaos, mass slaughter and corruption. In reality, the leaders of these revolutionary ideologies have political and financial motivations. They are resentful that the wealth and authority in the hands of the current rulers are not in their hands. They cloak their own motivations in religious rhetoric and through this innovated, political ideology, convince the youthful and ignorant who are not well-versed in Islāmic teachings that they are **individually obligated** to establish a caliphate which they believe is the only means to remove injustices being done to Muslims worldwide. Otherwise, they are told, they will be sinful and punished.[69]

This political ideology has parallels to 19th and 20th century Marxist revolutionary movements founded upon the slogan of "social justice" and has been clothed with religious rhetoric. This has been aptly noted by both Muslim scholars and Western academics.

---

[69] This viewpoint is based upon deep-rooted ignorance of the laws of God in his creation and the true causes behind calamities. By way of example, the Prophet said: "Never do the people cheat in weights and measures except that they are afflicted with years of hardship, scarcity of provision and the tyranny of the ruler." (Ṣaḥīḥ Ibn Mājah, no. 4019). Muslim scholars such as Ibn Taymiyyah and Ibn al-Qayyim expand upon this matter and explain that unjust, tyrannical rulers are simply a manifestation of the deeds of the subjects. Ibn al-Qayyim said: "For God, the Sublime, with His wisdom and justice makes the (consequences) of the actions of the servants to appear to them in forms that are appropriate to (those actions). So sometimes it is in the form of a drought or barrenness (of land). Other times it is by way of an enemy. Other times by way of tyrannical rulers. Other times by way of general diseases (that spread). Other times it is by anxiety, grief and worry that reside in their souls and do not leave them. Other times it is by preventing the blessings from the sky and the Earth from them." Zād al-Maʿād (4/363). Ibn Taymiyyah said, "Indeed, the affair (of rule) being destined for the kings and their deputies from the rulers, judges and leaders (who are unjust towards the people) is not due to deficiency in them alone, but due to the deficiency in both the shepherd and the flock together, for 'As you yourselves behave, you will be ruled over (in a like manner)' and God, the Exalted has said, '**Thus do we turn some of the oppressors against others on account of (the deeds) they earn**.' (6:129)." Majmūʿ al-Fatāwā (35/20-21). By involving Muslim masses in political activism and rousing their sentiments based upon ignorance of God's law with respect to the actions of his servants, misguided callers recruit sentimental Muslims into this revolutionary, caliphate-centric ideology of extremism which is not the legislated solution to the injustice and tyranny of rulers. This also shows that these people are ignorant of basic foundations of Islāmic theology and that they misquote and misrepresent the views of the scholars just cited.

The scholar, **Rabīʿ bin Hādī** said: "And this revolutionary ideology [of the modern Khārijites], we do not say it is 'influenced by the ideology of the Khārijites' but we say that it is influenced by the Communist, nationalist and secularist revolutions before it is influenced by the ideology of the Khārijites."[70] In his article titled, "How Marx Turned Muslim" for the Independent newspaper, Engish political philosopher **John Gray** wrote: "Islāmic fundamentalism is not an indigenous growth. It is an exotic hybrid, bred from the encounter of sections of the Islāmic intelligentsia with radical western ideologies. In 'A Fury for God', Malise Ruthven shows that Sayyid Qutb, an Egyptian executed after imprisonment in 1966 and arguably the most influential ideologue of radical Islām, incorporated many elements derived from European ideology into his thinking. For example, the idea of a revolutionary vanguard of militant believers does not have an Islāmic pedigree. It is 'a concept imported from Europe, through a lineage that stretches back to the Jacobins, through the Bolsheviks and latter-day Marxist guerrillas such as the Baader-Meinhof gang.' In a brilliantly illuminating and arrestingly readable analysis, Ruthven demonstrates the close affinities between radical Islamist thought and the vanguard of modernist and postmodern thinking in the West. The inspiration for Qutb's thought is not so much the Koran, but the current of western philosophy embodied in thinkers such as Nietzsche, Kierkegaard and Heidegger. Qutb's thought – the blueprint for all subsequent radical Islamist political theology – is as much a response to 20th-century Europe's experience of 'the death of God' as to anything in the Islāmic tradition. Qutbism is in no way traditional. Like all fundamentalist ideology, it is unmistakeably modern."[71]

Professor of Law **David Forte** wrote shortly after the September 11 attacks: "Over the past few weeks, I have argued that Osāma bin Lāden and his Taliban allies represent a perversion of Islam and are engaged in a campaign to change Islām itself to define the faith politically, and not primarily legally or theologically. The evidence, I believe, is unequivocal: His war is as much against Islam as it is against the West. I have written that Islam is a multivocal religion, that from its start it has debated within itself the nature of its identity. And I

---

[70] "Kashf al-Sitār" (pp. 32-33).

[71] "How Marx Turned Muslim", in the Independent, 27 July 2002.

have noted that among all its varied traditions, one thing remains clear: The acts of the terrorists of September 11, and the justification of them by Osāma bin Lāden, replicate in modern guise a violent faction, the Khārijites, that Islām found totally anathema to the faith early in its history. In other writings, I have asserted that this form of extremism has been inspired by the writings of influential modernist radicals, such as Sayyid Quṭb of Egypt, who believe that virtually all Islam is in a state of unbelief and needs to be re-conquered. Thus, in its modern form, Bin Lāden's kind of extremism has much more in common with Stalin, Hitler, and Mao than it does with Islāmic tradition. Like those state terrorists, Bin Lāden is at war with his own people. And finally, I have boldly asserted that bin Laden and his extremists are evil, pure and simple, and Islām is not. Since these opinions have been aired, I have received many letters, telephone calls, and e-mails. Without exception, Muslims who have contacted me have been grateful for my views. They have been relieved to hear how a Christian and Westerner is explaining to Americans the true nature of their religion. They have thanked me for my understanding of Islām. They agree with my characterization of Bin Lāden and al Qaeda."[72] From the above it is clear that this political ideology which draws from both the tradition of Marxist-Communist revolution and the doctrine of the very first sect, the Khārijite extremist renegades, has no basis in Islām.[73]

In a 2010 interview, French Professor **Olivier Roy**[74] was asked the question: "In your book you say that fundamentalist groups like al-Qaeda have nothing to do with Islāmic tradition. But in Europe the fundamentalist ideology is regarded as the essence of the traditional thinking. How do you explain this contradiction?" He answered: "The

---

[72] "Religion is Not the Enemy", The National Review, 19 October 2001.

[73] Academics and commentators offering the same analysis of Quṭb include Daniel Brogan, Ladan and Roya Boroumand, Paul Berman, Rod Dreher, Phil Paine, Lawrence Wright. They point out that Quṭb plagiarised Lenin's tract "What is to be done"? and simply used Islāmic terms to present a Leninist style revolution against Muslim governments. For more information refer to the book, "The Noble, Revered Prophet of Islām" (Hikmah Publications, 2015), a response to the attacks in Paris and the Charlie Hebdo cartoons.

[74] Olivier Roy is research director at the French National Centre for Scientific Research (CNRS) and lectures at the Ecole des Hautes Etudes en Sciences Sociales (EHESS) and the Institut d'Etudes Politiques (IEP) in Paris. He has numerous books on politics and Islām.

sort of terrorism practised by al-Qaeda has neither a Muslim nor a Christian history. It is an entirely new phenomenon. If we consider its manifestations – suicide bombing, killing hostages, targeting civilians – these are all methods that were used before al-Qaeda by other organisations: the Tamil Tigers, for example used suicide attacks; the extreme right in Italy was responsible for the Bologna bombing in August 1980; and the al-Qaeda video footage of the execution of foreign hostages in Iraq is a one to one 're-enactment' of the execution of Aldo Moro by the Red Brigades, with the organisation's banner and logo in the background, the hostage hand-cuffed and blind-folded, the mock 'trial' with the reading of the 'sentence' and the execution. Al-Qaeda's modus operandi and organisation, the declared enemy of US imperialism, the recruitment of young Muslims educated in the west or converts to Islam, **all this indicates clearly that al-Qaeda is not the expression of traditional Islam or even fundamentalist Islam; it is a new understanding of Islam, cloaked in western revolutionary ideology**."[75]

It is clear that this caliphate-centric ideology is rooted in the ideas of the Shiite and Khārijite sects and is strongly influenced by European revolutionary movements. It is unknown to orthodox Sunnī Muslims.

17. Are Muslims required to seek revenge?

The Prophet (peace be upon him) was sent as a mercy to mankind as stated by God: "**And we have not sent you except as a mercy to mankind**" (21:107). His success in the proclamation of his message would not have come about if he came as a fierce, vengeful, merciless warrior bent on domination. This is because people are naturally averse to the beliefs and values of those who behave with them in such ways.[76] On the contrary, the Prophet (peace be upon him) was the

---

[75] "When Religion and Culture Part Ways", 6 May 2010.

[76] This helps to explain the fact that wherever European powers colonised the lands of others for economic enrichment, they were always faced with sustained revolt from the indigenous people, forcing them in turn to wipe out hundreds of thousands to millions of "savages" and "barbarians." Examples include the indigenous populations of America, Australia and Africa. In contrast, indigenous populations were never wiped out by the spread of Islām which reached from Europe to Indonesia.

epitome of patience, forbearance and mercy. He never, ever sought revenge for personal reasons despite having the ability to do so on many occasions when his opponents were at his mercy. Despite the sustained oppression against his companions (many of whom were murdered), the assassination attempts on his life and the instigation of numerous wars against him, when he finally marched into Mecca to face those who opposed him for twenty-three years, he said to its 10,000 inhabitants, "You are free to go".

On one occasion, his companions asked him to supplicate against a particular tribe, the Daws, who had waged war against him. Instead he supplicated for them by asking God to bring them to him as believers. Towards the end of his life, the entire tribe accepted Islām. The Thaqīf tribe oppressed the Prophet and dishonoured him by having their children stone him until he bled and was expelled from their city. He was asked to supplicate against them but instead, he asked God to guide them. He also turned down an opportunity to have them punished and destroyed.

When Thumāmah, king of the region of al-Yamāmah, personally killed numerous Muslims and later set out to assassinate the Prophet, he was captured and brought to the Prophet who had him tied to the pillar of the mosque. He was left for three days whilst being provided food and drink and saw the prayer, humility, devotion and honour of the Muslims. He got an opportunity to see the daily practices of Muslims. When the Prophet spared his life and told him he was free to go, he barely reached the outskirts of Medina when he turned back, came to the Prophet and announced his Islām. The Meccan food supply was largely dependent upon the fertile region of al-Yamāmah and upon his return, as an eager convert, Thumāmah cut off all food supplies to the polytheists of Mecca to punish them for their oppression and disgraceful behaviour towards the Prophet. The Meccans lodged a complaint to the Prophet knowing full well that they themselves had socially and economically boycotted the Prophet and his followers for a period of three years. As a result, the Prophet and his companions had been forced to live in valleys and survive by eating the leaves of trees or food that was smuggled to them by sympathetic non-Muslim relatives. The Prophet ordered Thumāmah to lift the boycott against the Meccans, the very ones who had attempted to assassinate him, expelled him from his home, murdered his companions and starved him and his followers.

These are only a few illustrations of the mercy, kindness and compassion of the Prophet of Islām. The hearts were not won by the sword but by the superior moral character of the Prophet and his abundant mercy. This shows that the Muslim who follows the way of the Prophet cannot be motivated by personal or worldly reasons, since his intent is not to harm people nor to seek revenge, but to facilitate every way for their guidance and betterment.

Angry, disaffected Muslims who hold hatred in their hearts towards the ordinary, innocent citizens of European nations that colonised Muslim lands and who justify acts of terrorism against them are not following the guidance and example of the Prophet (peace be upon him). They are consumed by toxic emotions and sentiments that inspire feelings of revenge whereas the Prophet never harboured such feelings.[77] Rather, he desired guidance and enlightenment for the people. The millions of people living in Britain and Europe today are not responsible for the depraved and horrendous colonialist crimes of those who preceded them.[78] The vast majority of the people in these

---

[77] In the 1099 capture of Jerusalem, the European Crusaders mercilessly slaughtered the city's Muslim and Jewish inhabitants until the streets flowed with blood. In contrast, Ṣalāḥuddīn, the Muslim leader who recaptured Jerusalem in 1187, spared the lives of 100,000 Christians and gave them free passage along with their property and belongings. This compassionate act, along with his bravery and chivalry in war, won him great respect and he continues to be spoken of with praise and adulation by non-Muslims.

[78] By way of example, within three decades of entering Algeria in the mid to late 19th century the French Military massacred one million Algerians, wiping out one third of the entire population. This murderous rampage continued right into the mid-20th century and their atrocities included rape, molestation of young girls and married women, cutting off the heads of their victims and parading them as trophies (pictures of which are readily available online), wiping out entire villages and towns of tens of thousands at a time and more. Much has been has documented and written on this subject. One can refer to the essay of Joseph Massad, a Palestinian Christian, titled, "Assimilating French Muslims", 22 January 2015, and numerous detailed papers written by Asafa Jalata, Professor of Sociology at the University of Tennessee, Knoxville on the subject of colonialist genocide in general. These atrocities are mentioned here only to make it clear that Western nations do not have any high moral ground when combating modern manifestations of terrorism. The capacity to commit organised, brutal mass-murder for ideological grounds, self-

countries do not support adventurous conflicts in foreign lands or the killing of Muslims. In fact, millions of non-Muslims march in the streets of capitals to protest against participation in such wars.[79] They are more in need of having a sound, authentic understanding of Islām to help remove whatever misconceptions and prejudices they may harbour than they are of being attacked and harmed for things for which they bear no responsibility whatsoever.

18. Do Muslims have to forcibly convert non-Muslims to Islām?

Forced conversion is strictly forbidden in Islām. Genuine belief has to be voluntary. The Qur'ān states, "**There is no compulsion in religion**." (2:256). The Muslim scholar, Ibn al-Qayyim (d. 1350) elaborated: "This verse was revealed regarding some men amongst the Companions [of the Prophet]. They had children who had become Jews and Christians prior to Islām. When Islām came, their fathers accepted Islām and they desired to compel their children upon the religion. So they were prohibited from that by God, the Sublime, so that they themselves could [willingly] choose to enter into Islām. That which is correct [regarding this verse] is that upon its generality of meaning, it applies to every non-Muslim... It will become clear to whoever reflects upon the biographical account of the Prophet (peace be upon him) that he did not compel a single person to accept his religion, ever."[80] Islām was not spread by the sword, this is a myth that has persisted through the centuries. We cited earlier the statements of **Lawrence Browne**, **James Michener** and **De Lacy O'Leary** in this regard who made clear that this is "one of the most fantastically absurd myths that historians have ever repeated."[81] The entire Arabian peninsula accepted Islām at the cost of only 800 to 900 lives during an 8 year period. These lives were lost only because the Prophet was forced to participate in wars due to aggression being initiated against him. His followers were

---

enrichment or a combination of both, can be found in humans when the right circumstances and opportunities are present. It is not unique to any religion or belief system, but returns to the **instrinsic, oppressive, greedy nature of man**.

[79] "'Million' March Against Irāq War", BBC News, 16 February 2003.

[80] Ḥidāyat al-Hayārā, Dār ʿĀlam al-Fawā'id, p. 29.

[81] Refer to the section, "Who Was Muḥammad?" earlier in this book.

expelled from their homes, their wealth and livelihood was confiscated, many of them were tortured and murdered, and numerous alliances were formed to destroy the entire Muslim community. Muslims are encouraged to be beacons of light for Islām and invite others to the simplicity and beauty of its message and teachings through exemplary conduct, beautiful admonition and arguing in ways which are best. The inherent power in the simplicity, beauty and naturalness of its message is enough to capture honest and sincere hearts without the need for forced conversion.

19. Are Muslims required to engage in subversive "jihād"?

The word jihāḍ refers to a "struggle" of any kind in which a Muslim strives to better himself in terms of piety, righteousness, moral character and mannerisms out of obedience to God. It includes striving with one's soul, one's heart, one's body and one's wealth and applies to all arenas of life. The Prophet (peace be upon him) said, "The mujāhid (one engaged in jihād) is the one who struggles against his own soul in obedience to God." One of the loftiest forms of jihād is serving one's parents in their old age. Likewise, waging war against the deviants and extremists such as the Khārijite terrorists is from the loftiest forms of jihād. Another form of jihād is showing resolve and patience when afflicted with calamities such as poverty, hunger and illness. Another form of jihād is to raise daughters with kind treatment for which the Prophet (peace be upon him) specified great reward.

From its outward manifestations is the jihād of fighting (qitāl). This takes the form of legitimate, just warfare whose objective is to remove aggression against the peaceful proclamation and practice of Islām, to protect its adherents from tribulation and to establish justice. All nations assume the right to wage war for the protection of their values, wealth and land in order to preserve national security. However, it should be made clear that war in Islām is not a war of colonialism, nor is it a war of economies or to dispossess people of their land, property and wealth. Nor is to globalize trade or open up "free markets." Nor is it to extract minerals, metals and fuels from usurped land. Nor is it to display the superiority of one's tribe, race or nation. God said: "**That home of the Hereafter We assign to those who do not desire exaltedness upon the earth or corruption. And the [best] outcome is for the**

righteous." (28:83). Pursuing greatness in authority and causing corruption on Earth is prohibited. It is the way of the tyrants, warmongers and nation-destroyers.[82]

Jihād is regulated, has strict conditions and cannot be announced and waged haphazardly by individuals, vigilantes or insurgent groups. That which is done by al-Qaeda, ISIS, the Ṭālibān and Boko Ḥarām is not jihād but corruption motivated by political, social and economic factors. It has no connection to the honourable and dignified concept of jihād in Islām, even if it is clothed in the garment of Islām and made to appear as such. Jihād is announced and performed only under the leadership of the Muslim ruler and his government[83] when he sees that engaging in jihād is necessary for the beneficial interests of the state

---

[82] As for the jihād of the Prophet, the famous scholar, Ibn al-Qayyim (d. 1350) explains: "It will become clear to whoever reflects upon the biographical account of the Prophet (peace be upon him) that he did not compel a single person to accept his religion, ever. Rather, he fought whoever fought against him [first]. As for the one who made a truce with him, he never fought him so long as that person remained upon the truce and did not violate his covenant. Rather, God Almighty commanded the Prophet to fulfil the covenant with them, so long as they abided by it, just as He, the Exalted said, '**So as long as they are upright toward you, be upright toward them**' (9:7). When he came to Medina he made peace treaties with the Jews and affirmed them upon their religion. When they waged war against him by breaking their covenant and initiating fighting against him, only then did he fight against them. Thereafter he showed favour to some of them (sparing them), exiled others and killed others [with just cause]. Likewise when he made a truce with the Quraysh for ten years, he never initiated fighting against them until they initiated fighting against him and violated their covenant. When they did that, he fought against them in their lands. Prior to that, they had fought against him, such as when they desired [to kill] him on the day of Uḥud and the day of the Battle of the Trench and the day of Badr as well. They came to fight against him [first], but if they had turned away from him [and left him] he would not have fought them. The intent here is that he (peace be upon him) never compelled anyone to enter his religion, ever. Rather, the people entered his religion wilfully, out of choice. The majority of the people of the Earth entered his call when guidance became clear to them and that He is the Messenger of God in truth." Ḥidāyat al-Hayārā (Dār 'Ālam al-Fawā'id) pp. 29-30.

[83] We have already established that ISIS is not a legitimate Muslim authority but rather a group of bandits and renegades who have inherited the doctrine of the Khārijites. These renegades are to be fought in every age and era by legitimate Muslim authorities as per the Prophetic traditions.

and its subjects. It is fought honourably, without treachery and for the sake of God. It is not waged for land, wealth, power, fame, chivalry, nationalism, or revenge. Only combatants are to be fought and as for women, children, the elderly, those devoted to worship such as priests and monks, they are not allowed to be killed. The destruction of infrastructure and means of livelihood is prohibited. Captives are to be treated with benevolence and looked after through housing, clothing, food and drink. Further, Muslim rulers may enter into peace treaties as a means of warding off or ending hostilities and these agreements must be strictly honoured. Decisions about war, peace, covenants and other relations are only made by the ruler and his government.

In contrast to the orderly and just manner in which jihād is performed honourably in accordance with Islāmic principles for lofty objectives, the Khārijite bandits distort and overturn this lofty institution and use it as a tool of chaos, turmoil and mass slaughter, primarily against Muslim societies. Operating as insurgents who have no legitimate Islāmic authority, they are driven by wealth, authority, personal grievances and revenge, cloaking all of this with religious rhetoric. They recruit the foolish and ignorant, brainwashing them into thinking they are making jihād in the path of God, when in reality, it is jihād in the path of Satan. For this reason, the famous Muslim scholar, **Ibn Taymiyyah** (d. 1328) remarked: "It is obligatory to know the legislated jihād which was commanded by God and His Messenger from the innovated jihād of the people of misguidance who make jihād in obeying Satan whilst they think they are making jihād in obeying the Most Gracious, such as the Khārijites and their likes who make jihād against the people of Islām."[84]

Some examples of legitimate jihād include the expulsion of Soviet Russian occupying forces from Afghānistān. This jihād was supported by many Muslim governments at the time and had clear direction and leadership. However, Egyptian elements spread their extremist Takfīrī ideology amongst its participants and this led to subsequent chaos and turmoil in Afghānistān. Likewise, the war against Ṣaddām Ḥussain, a Baʿthist, who occupied Kuwait in 1990 and threatened the borders of Saudi Arabia which were defended through the Islāmically permissible use of alliances and third-party forces. The audacious move by

[84] "Al-Radd ʿalā al-Akhnaʾī" (p. 205).

Ṣaddām Hussain to attack and annex Kuwait led to tribulations for the Irāqī nation which have not ceased till this day. Another example of jihād is the formation in December 2015 of an alliance of thirty-five Muslim countries to combat terrorism and the Khārijite ideology that drives it. This amounts to acting upon the command of the Prophet (peace be upon him) to fight the Khārijites wherever they appear. Likewise, it is acting upon the sayings of prominent Muslim scholars such as Ibn Taymiyyah who stated that the Khārijites are primary targets of the legislated Jihād which can be initiated against them even if they do not commence fighting first.[85]

20. Are Muslims required to establish Islāmic Law in Britain and Europe?

Firstly, caliphate-centric groups such as Ḥizb al-Taḥrīr originally operated in Muslim countries on the basis of their Khārijite ideology that those countries are lands of disbelief. They believe that only by taking power and establishing Islāmic law can those lands be considered Islāmic again. When they met with very little success in those countries a point of discussion arose as to whether their call could be implemented in non-Muslim countries as well. According to them, Muslim countries were no different than non-Muslim countries as both were considered abodes of disbelief (dār kufr) and practically the same. In the late 80s and early 90s, Ḥizb al-Taḥrīr appeared on the scene in Britain and began recruiting through universities and mosques. **Omar Bakrī** was an instrumental figure in creating this group and advancing its goals. His student **Anjem Choudary**, is currently the main representative of this ideology in the UK. They have counterparts in other places such as France, Holland, Belgium and elsewhere. Due to the sustained efforts of Salafī Muslims in Britain in refuting this deviant ideology during the 1990s and 2000s this group relied upon concealment and dissimulation and started operating under a variety of different names and identities. Most recently, they have assumed the "Salafist" label as their latest instance of deception and camouflage. **Secondly**, snatching power is the political ideology of the Khārijites as has preceded and is not what Islām calls to. It is prohibited, even if the rulers are tyrannical and unjust. **Thirdly**, Islāmic Law considers the

[85] "Al-Siyāsah al-Shar'iyyah" (Dār 'Ālam al-Fawā'id) pp. 161, 163.

arrangement of Muslims living under non-Muslim rule in which there is a guarantee of protection to be a contractual agreement which must be honoured and not violated.[86] **Fourthly**, given the political, legal and economic structures, the highly-organised and efficient police, military and intelligence services in these countries, an unwilling population of tens of millions and treaties between countries, trying to "establish a caliphate" in these lands is a sign of madness. The people upon this ideology are nothing but a tiny group of loudmouth fantasists inspired by hallucinations of a "caliphate" in the UK or other European countries. Governments, intelligence agencies and smart political analysts know this full well. **Fifthly**, nevertheless, since their roots lie in Khārijite ideology, they do have the effect of radicalising naive, ignorant Muslims and drawing them towards terrorist groups like ISIS. This is a dangerous matter that must be addressed in an effective way. This includes educating ordinary Muslims about the sources of this ideology and its conflict with Islām and explaining to them that it is sinful to join these groups or adopt their ideology. **Sixthly**, their controversial, provocative, fruitless activities provide fuel for the Neoconservatives and right-wing movements who work to shape public opinion against Muslims in general to further their political agendas. **Seventhly**, since the 1980s dubious figures such as **Muḥammad al-Misʿarī** (Ḥizb al-Taḥrīr), **Omar Bakrī** (Ḥizb al-Taḥrīr), **Saʿd al-Faqīh** and others who are upon the caliphate ideology have been given asylum and protection in Britain. They are dissidents from Saudi Arabia who were involved in seditious activities against the government, considering it an apostate state. Upon reaching the shores of Britain, they started calling to their extremist ideology and affected a generation of youth. Today, the ones being recruited to join ISIS are from this same generation. They all have backgrounds in the ideology of Ḥizb al-Taḥrīr whose offshoots include al-Muhājiroun, Islām4UK and others. They are neither "Wahhābists" nor Salafists and they never took knowledge or studied with the contemporary Salafī scholars. When one analyses the religious backgrounds of those who travel to Syria to join ISIS, an

---

[86] This is based upon the fact that when Muslims were persecuted in Mecca, they emigrated to Abysinnia and lived under Negus, the Christian ruler. The Muslims lived honourably and peacefully and did not cause sedition or turmoil.

extremely high percentage are those poisoned by the Ḥizb al-Taḥrīr, caliphate-centric ideology which goes under different names and labels in various European countries such as Britain, Germany, France, Holland and Belgium.[87] **Eighthly**, contrary to the lies of this group, Muslims living under contract in non-Muslim lands with a guarantee of safety, welfare and protection have no authority to "establish Islāmic law". This requirement is for a Muslim ruler and his government in relation to matters of crime, economy, politics and national security. **Ninthly**, in reality, these people are nothing but an extension of 19th and 20th century Marxist, Communist revolutionary movements save that alongside the slogans of "political", "social" and "economic justice", they have added the religious rhetoric of the Khārijite renegades. The founder of Ḥizb al-Taḥrīr, **Taqī al-Dīn al-Nabhānī**, was a Baʿthist nationalist. He was involved in revolutionary activities in Syria and Jordan before setting up this group which was but an extension of his prior activities clothed in Islāmic garb.

---

[87] By way of example, Belgium is a relatively small country but proportionally speaking it has supplied a large number of Jihādists. According to reports, a higher percentage of Muslims in Belgium travelled to Syria than Muslims of Britain, Germany, France or Holland. The group responsible for shaping their views was **Shariah4Belgium**, whose ideology is that of Ḥizb al-Taḥrīr. The head of this group is **Abu Imrān Fouad Belkacem** of Moroccan parents. He was heavily influenced and helped by Anjem Choudary and his group in Britain. It is reported that Belkacem travelled to London to seek advice from Choudary on how to start an organisation in Belgium. This organisation became popular in Belgium and most or possibly even all Belgians who have gone to Syria are connected with them. They also influenced Dutch Muslim youth and started a Dutch organisation named **Shariah4Holland**. Most Dutch Syria-fighters were in contact with Shariah4Belgium. The pattern is the same in Britain. Active recruiters for ISIS all have a background in the ideology of Ḥizb al-Taḥrīr and have been affiliated with its various front-organisations such as al-Muhājiroun, Islām4UK and others. It must be made clear that these are not "Wahhābist" or Salafist groups. Some of them have deceptively assumed the Salafist label over the past 5-7 years because they found it a convenient means of concealing their true identity and underlying ideology. In actual reality, they excommunicate all the Salafī scholars of today and the Salafīs have been exposing them since the 1980s with a long trail of refutations. The refutations against the charlatan Omar Bakrī during the 1990s are well known to those who are familiar with the events of that time period.

21. What are the obligations of Muslims in non-Muslim lands?

The duties and obligations of Muslims who live in non-Muslim countries are clearly outlined by Muslim scholars on the basis of texts that relate to contractual obligations.

The late and well-known Salafī scholar of Saudi Arabia **Muḥammad bin Ṣāliḥ al-'Uthaymīn** (d. 2001) advised a large gathering of Muslims in the United Kingdom via tele-link in July 2000: "I invite you to have respect for those people who have the right that they should be respected, those with whom there is an agreement [of protection] for you. For the land in which you are living is such that there is an agreement between you and them. If this were not the case they would have killed you or expelled you. So preserve this agreement, and do not prove treacherous to it, since treachery is a sign of the hypocrites, and it is not from the way of the believers. And know that it is authentically reported from the Prophet that he said, 'Whoever kills [a non-Muslim] who is under an agreement of protection will not smell the fragrance of Paradise.' Do not be fooled by the sayings of those foolish people, those who say 'These people are non-Muslims, so their wealth is lawful for us [to misappropriate or take by way of murder and killing].' For by God, this is a lie. A lie about God's religion, and a lie about Islāmic societies. We cannot say that it is lawful to be treacherous towards people whom we have an agreement with. O my brothers, O youth, O Muslims, be truthful in your buying and selling, and renting, and leasing, and in all mutual transactions. Because truthfulness is from the characteristics of the believers, and God, Blessed and Exalted, has commanded truthfulness in His saying, '**O you who believe, fear and keep your duty to God and be with the truthful**' (9:119). And the Prophet encouraged truthfulness and said, 'Adhere to truthfulness, because truthfulness leads to goodness, and goodness leads to Paradise. And a person will continue to be truthful, and strive to be truthful until he will be written down with God as a truthful person.' And he warned against falsehood, and said, 'Beware of falsehood, because falsehood leads to wickedness, and wickedness leads to the Fire. And a person will continue lying, and striving to lie until he is written down with God as a great liar.' O my brother Muslims, O youth, be true in your sayings with your brothers, and with those non-Muslims whom you live along amongst so that you will be true inviters to the religion of Islām by your actions. So how many people there are who first entered into Islām because of the behaviour and manners of the Muslims, their truthfulness and being true in their dealings."[88]

Another scholar, **Rabīʿ bin Hādī** stated: "From the greatest and most-distinguished qualities enjoined by Islām is the fulfilment of covenants and the fulfilment of contracts and promises, even with the non-Muslims. And from the traits of the believers is the absence of treachery. Hence, it is upon the Muslims to be the striking example in truthfulness, lofty manners, fulfilment of trusts and to remain far away from these attributes of treachery, perfidy, deception, lying and taking life which does not benefit Islām but harms Islām."[89]

The late Salafī scholar, **Aḥmad bin Yaḥyā al-Najmī** (d. 2008) said: "The Prophet (peace be upon him) would prohibit perfidy and treachery and he would command with truthfulness, innocence and trustworthiness. As for what the terrorists do in this time when they wear bombs or they drive cars loaded with bombs and on finding a gathering of people they blow themselves up or the blow the car up, then this practice is built upon deception, Islām is far, far away from this and does not affirm it at all. What is being done now of suicide missions in Britain or other lands, they are planned and executed by the Takfīrī Khārijites, These people are from the organisation of al-Qaeda, those who follow Osāma bin Lādin, [Muḥammad] al-Misʿarī and Saʿd al-Faqīh and their likes who have been nurtured upon the books of thinkers (and not genuine scholars) such as Sayyid Quṭb."[90]

The Salafī scholar, **Muḥammad bin Hādī**, in his outstanding lecture dated 13th May 2014 in the city of Medina, exhorted the 200 or so mostly Western attendees to adhere to truthfulness (ṣidq) in their dealings, contracts, and agreements with non-Muslims. Likewise he enjoined gentleness (rifq) and also encouraged humility (tawāḍuʿ), illustrating each of these three traits through practical examples from the Prophet Muḥammad (peace be upon him). This is the reality of Islām, it places tremendous value on honouring one's contracts and displaying the peak of perfection in human character.

---

[88] From a tele-link recording on 28 July 2000 at a conference organised by Salafī Publications (Maktabah Salafiyyah) in the city of Birmingham.

[89] Abridged, from the cassette "Verdicts of the Scholars on Assassinations and Bombings" Tasjīlāt Minhāj al-Sunnah, Riyāḍ.

[90] In a dictated statement issued following the 2005 London 7/7 attacks.

22. Are devout Muslims a threat to safety and security?

Devout Muslims who understand their faith well and hold fast to its teachings which demand **justice in dealings** with all people pose no threat at all to the safety and security of the societies they live in. Such people are buffered by their faith from committing actions that Islām prohibits severely and condemns such as theft, taking intoxicants and drugs, crimes of a sexual nature such as kidnap, rape, murder, organised crime and terrorism. An article in the Guardian titled, "MI5 report challenges views on terrorism in Britain", notes the following: "Far from being religious zealots, a large number of those involved in terrorism do not practise their faith regularly. Many lack religious literacy and could actually be regarded as religious novices. Very few have been brought up in strongly religious households, and there is a higher than average proportion of converts. Some are involved in drug-taking, drinking alcohol and visiting prostitutes. **MI5 says there is evidence that a well-established religious identity actually protects against violent radicalisation**."[91] This is a true statement and the empirical evidence from the studies of knowledgeable devout Muslims and ignorant sinful Muslims validates it.

As **Karen Armstrong**, a famous author on comparative religion with many books on Islām stated: "There have been surveys done by forensic psychiatrists who interviewed people convicted of terrorism since 9/11. They interviewed hundreds of people in Guantanamo and other prisons. And one forensic psychiatrist who is also an officer of the CIA concluded that Islam had nothing to do with it. The problem is rather ignorance of the Islām. Had they had a proper Muslim education they wouldn't be doing this. Only 20% of them has had a regular Muslim upbringing. The rest are either new converts like the gunmen who recently attacked the Canadian Parliament; or non-observant, which means they don't go to the mosque, like the bombers in the Boston marathon; or self-taught. Two young men who left Britain to join the Jihād in Syria ordered from Amazon a book called Islam for Dummies. That says it, you see."[92]

---

[91] http://www.theguardian.com/uk/2008/aug/20/uksecurity.terrorism1

[92] Online interview with Dutch paper, Nieuwwij.nl, 18 January 2015.

So called "religious extremism" arises due to abandonment of the moderate, balanced and just guidance of the Prophet Muḥammad (peace be upon him) and not because of following it. Speaking of religious extremism, the Prophet said: "The extremists have perished, the extremists have perished, the extremists have perished." Upon learning that some men were intending to exaggerate in prayer, fasting and practise celibacy he informed them: "Whoever turns away from my tradition is not from me."[93] He also said: "By God, he does not have faith, by God, he does not have faith, by God, he does not have faith whose neighbour is not safe from his harm." Under the chapter heading, "The Jewish Neighbour", the famous collector of Prophetic traditions, Imām al-Bukhārī (d. 870) relates the following authentic tradition from the commentator of the Qur'ān, Mujāhid (d. 722), who said: "I was with ʿAbdullāh bin ʿAmr (a companion of the Prophet) whilst his servant was preparing a sheep for a meal and he said, 'O servant! When you have finished cooking the meal then begin by offering to our Jewish neighbour first. I heard the Prophet advising with kindness to the neighbour with such emphasis until we feared he would relate to us [through revelation] that the neighbour is to inherit from his fellow neighbour'."[94] A man said to the Prophet (peace be upon him) that a particular woman is mentioned with plentiful prayer, charity and fasting but she abuses her neighbour with her tongue. The Prophet said, "She is in the Hellfire." Then the man said that a particular woman is mentioned with little prayer, fasting and charity, but she gives the cheese of oxen in charity and does not harm her neighbour. The Prophet said, "She is in Paradise."[95]

Even animals, trees and the environment have rights upon Muslims which must be fulfilled and not violated. Hence, there is no reason to be scared of devout, practising Muslims who proceed upon knowledge and insight in their religion. By their knowledge and devoutness, they are buffered from radicalisation and extremism. Their stable religious observance separates them from unstable Muslims who live a life of vice and crime and in their remorseful state become prone to easy recruitment into radical ideology by extremists who exploit their desire for penitence and severe lack of Islāmic knowledge. Thus, when you

---

[93] Related by al-Bukhārī.

[94] Related by al-Bukhārī in "al-Adab al-Mufrad."

[95] Related by al-Bukhārī in "al-Adab al-Mufrad", al-Bayhaqī and others.

see a bearded Muslim or a woman wearing hijāb, it is unjust to hold unwarranted suspicions about them. Unless there are clear signs of the extremist ideology whose details have been outlined in this book, it is counterproductive to hold negative opinions about ordinary, devout Muslims and does little to combat actual extremism.

23. Are sinful Muslims acting on Islāmic teachings?

It ought to be obvious to any reasonable person that the actions of those of Muslim backgrounds who commit crimes which Islām condemns and for which it specifies very severe punishments cannot be attributed to Islām. Muslims in Western nations who are engaged in selling drugs, organised crime, grooming, rape and prostitution, if they were convicted of the same crimes in a Muslim country such as Saudi Arabia, they would be meted out justice with capital punishment and most likely with the death penalty. It is therefore ludicrous and a blatant sign of bias when these evil criminals in Western lands are routinely identified in media reports as "Muslims" and "Islāmic", as if their crimes are sanctioned by the Qur'ān and the Prophetic traditions. This only incites unsophisticated, extremist right-wing elements and creates even more unwanted tension in societies. In contrast, religious identity is rarely made prominent in provocative headlines when similar crimes are committed by those from other backgrounds.

24. What are the signs of radical extremists?

Governments of Western nations are increasingly trying to devise their own version of Islām which they wish to enforce upon Muslims as a means of "combating extremism." Based on dubious guidelines, educators across schools, colleges, universities and other institutions are being led to consider praying regularly, fasting in Ramaḍān, growing a beard, wearing a hijāb or headscarf and other standard Islāmic practices as signs of "extremism" and "radical ideology." As a result, the number of Muslims being referred to the authorities for alleged radicalisation has increased exponentially. A culture of suspicion is being fermented through pea-brained policies which do little if anything to address the true underlying causes behind extremist and terrorist ideology.

We present here a number of genuine criteria that will immediately identify an extremist: **a)** claiming that all contemporary Muslim rulers have left Islām and that their governments must be removed, **b)** constantly attacking the rulers and scholars of the Muslims, abusing them and blaming them for all the woes of the Muslim world, **c)** demanding that Muslim governments cut off all trade and diplomatic ties with non-Muslim governments, **d)** claiming that establishment of the caliphate is the primary objective of Islām and is an individual obligation upon every Muslim, **e)** possessing and reading the works and writings of Sayyid Quṭb, Taqī al-Dīn al-Nabhānī and others mentioned in this book, **f)** praising, supporting and defending groups like al-Qaeda and ISIS, their heads and ideologues such as Abū Bakr al-Baghdadī, Osama bin Lādin, Ayman al-Zawāhrī, Abū Qatādah, Abū Muḥammad al-Maqdisī, Anwar al-Awlakī and others, **g)** glorifying acts of terrorism as "jihād", **h)** blaming the populations of non-Muslim countries for crimes and atrocities they are innocent of and do not condone, **i)** claiming jihād is an individual obligation upon every single Muslim in the world and does not require consent of leaders and parents, **j)** gloating at the death of innocent, non-Muslim civilians and belittling the death of Muslims killed by the terrorists and **k)** facilitating or providing material assistance to others to join and travel to groups such as ISIS. These views and activities are a natural extension of the extremist Khārijite ideology we have discussed in detail in this book. On the other hand, outward signs of a practicing, observant Muslim can never be used on their own to suspect extremism.[96]

25. Is there a campaign to spread hatred against Muslims?

There are numerous orientations and groups whose interests are served by hatemongering against Islām and Muslims. Criminal acts

---

[96] The UK government's PREVENT program to combat extremism has been criticised for both failing and being hijacked by the Neoconservatives and their political agendas. It has been alleged to have turned into a Muslim witch-hunt program involving organised monitoring (spying) and profiling. The vague, undefined, catchall term "non violent extremism" is said to be behind this policy which fuels suspicion and hate and does little to address the true and real causes of extremism. Evidence is also said to exist of an organised form of entrapment that has been implemented within some schools to draw Muslim children into being classified as "potential radicals". If true, these approaches are counterproductive and lead to resentment and distrust.

performed by those of Muslim backgrounds are frequently employed to paint a specific picture about Islām despite the fact that those acts are specifically condemned in Islām's primary texts and are subject to capital punishments.

With respect to **the first group**, David Miller, Professor of Sociology at the University of Strathclyde, wrote a 70 page report titled "The Cold War on British Muslims" on the role of conservative organisations and think-tanks such as **Policy Exchange** and **Centre for Social Cohesion (CSC)** in stirring sentiments and hatred against Muslims in Britain. The report reveals the sources of funding, tracing them to Zionist organisations.[97] A similar situation exists in the United States as revealed in the detailed report titled "Fear Inc. The Roots of the Islamophobia Network in America"[98] by the Center for American Progress Action Fund. It shows how $42 million from seven pro-Zionist foundations are behind the rise of Islamophobia in America. A slick, sophisticated and well-organised network exists to channel hatred into the hearts and minds of Americans through the media. This network starts with the pro-Zionist donors who channel large amounts of funds to the tune of tens of millions. The next level consists of key **misinformation experts** such as Frank Gaffney, David Yerushalmi, Robert Spencer and Steven Emerson (the fraudulent pseudo-expert

---

[97] From the report: "We wrote to Policy Exchange and the CSC requesting, in the interests of transparency, that they disclose its sources of funding. The CSC stated in its response only that it was funded by private donations and has 'neither sought nor received public funds'. Policy Exchange failed to respond. Nevertheless, our report reveals for the first time the network of individuals and foundations that are bankrolling both think-tanks. Donors identified in the report include the neoconservative Rosenkranz Foundation in the United States, and hardline Zionists such as Stanley Kalms and the late Cyril Stein in the UK. It reveals that both think-tanks share major donors with a number of controversial organisations – including the Association for the Wellbeing of Israel's Soldiers, the Israel-Diaspora Trust (an organisation founded by the late Rabbi Sidney Brichto, a passionate supporter of Israel and scourge of its critics inside and outside the UK Jewish community) and the Anglo-Israel Association, founded in 1949 by the Christian Zionist Sir Wyndham Deedes. His nephew William Deedes became an editor of the Daily Telegraph and, in 2006, wrote an opinion piece entitled: 'Muslims can never conform to our ways'." The full report can be downloaded from the website http://www.spinwatch.org.

[98] http://www.americanprogress.org/issues/2011/08/pdf/islamophobia.pdf

who claimed Birmingham was a complete no-go area for non-Muslims in Britain). The misinformation created by this small nucleus is then passed through **four echo chambers** to reach the public. They are **the religious right** in the form pro-Zionist Christians such as Pat Robertson, John Hagee, Ralph Reed and Franklin Graham. Secondly, **political figures** such as Allen West, Michelle Bachman, Renee Elmers and others. Thirdly, **media organisations** and figures such as Fox News, Clarion Fund, Washington Times, Sean Hannity, Glenn Beck, Pamela Geller by way of example only. And fourthly, **grassroots campaign organisations** operating under the cloak of human and women's rights. These groups amplify the misinformation and instill suspicion, fear and hatred into the hearts of hundreds of millions of people against Muslims.[99] This propaganda is also connected to the injustices against Muslims in Palestine and serves to prevent widespread negative public opinion from taking shape against these injustices.

It must be made clear that very large numbers of Jews all across the world, both religious and secular, deplore the actions of religious and political Zionists in oppressing the Palestinians by occupying the lands they inhabited for centuries and forcing them to live in what can only amount to prison-like conditions.[100] Hardline Zionists have been known to portray Islām and Muslims as a threat to any country they reside in as an indirect means of justifying oppression against the Palestinian population, coercing unwilling Jews to move to Israel and advancing their long-term expansionist policies in the region. Millions of Jews who live happily in their host countries across the world are resistant to attempts by hardline Zionists to coerce them to migrate to Israel. Ultra-orthodox Jews and organisations such as Neturei Karta, or "Orthodox Jews United Against Zionism", are active campaigners against religious Zionism which they believe is an innovated political ideology that has hijacked Judaism to the detriment of the Jewish people.

Some view this ideology similar to how the Khārijite ideology is viewed by mainstream Muslims: Visions of an exclusive Jewish state (caliphate) led by religious supremacist extremists (renegades) engaged in violent aggressive war (jihād) against the "Amalekites" with

---

[99] For a summary of the report refer to http://thkpr.gs/qrznnx.

[100] A long-standing outspoken critic of the brutal crimes perpetrated against Palestinians is **Gerald Kaufman**, former Zionist and veteran Labour MP.

a view of total annihilation of all enemies and taking hold of their lands, homes and possessions. These enemies include "apostate" Jewish "traitors" (such as the assassinated Yitzakh Rabin) who make peace, not war, with the enemy. One only need to read the essay "**18 Principles of Rebirth**" as outlined by Avraham Stern, (founder of the terrorist group Lehi, known as the "Stern Gang"), to identify this way of thinking which has parallels with the caliphate-centric ideas of ISIS. Israel Shahak's "Jewish Fundamentalism in Israel"[101] is an eye-opening read on the role and influence of Jewish religious extremists such as **Gush Emunim** and the **Haredis** in the politics of the region.

The second group is the network of evangelical fundamentalist Christians allied to the Zionists. They exist mostly in the United States and believe that annihilation of Arab Muslims is a requirement for the Messianic end times to be ushered in. They believe that only after Israel is established and victorious over the Arabs will Jesus return and every Jew will then be converted to Christianity and will accept that Jesus is his saviour who died for his sins.[102]

As more and more people of educated, Western backgrounds learn about the simplicity, rationality and coherence in the basic Islāmic creed, how it provides clear, unambiguous moral direction and accept Islām as their way of life, evangelical fundamentalists use large-scale propaganda methods in pursuit of their agendas. Hatemongering against Islām and Muslims is one of their major activities. Because they have a very large following, especially in America, along with lots of wealth and reach, they play an instrumental role in spreading hate and fear by misrepresenting Islām. They engage in deeply polemical

---

[101] Pluto Press, 2004. Israel Shahak, an Israeli professor at the Hebrew University of Jerusalem, was a liberal, secular thinker.

[102] Muslims reject the idea that a man has to throw his son in front of a bus or feed him to the sharks and then say to his unjust neighbours, "I love you so much that I sacrificed my begotten son for you. All you have to do is believe that I sacrificed my son who died for your transgressions against me and you will receive my mercy, forgiveness and grace." To ascribe this to a man is to insult him. To ascribe this to God is an even greater insult in the view of Muslims who venerate God as the all-Forgiving and all-Merciful. God forgives when a person shows remorse for his or her sin, seeks forgiveness and repents. There is no need for blood sacrifices. These are Pagan concepts and are foreign to the teachings of the Prophets of God.

methods in which studies of Islāmic beliefs, principles and laws are made in order to misconstrue and portray them in the worst possible light, stripped of the spirit of the law behind them and the objectives and wisdoms attached to them. This provides them with a layer of obfuscation and misdirection by which their audiences are prevented from comparing the confusing, contradictory theology of Christianity with the simplicity and coherence of the Islāmic treatment of divinity, faith and salvation.

The third group consists of right-wing xenophobic elements mainly across Europe but also in the United States. At the higher level, they include certain political parties and at the lower level there are groups such as Pegida in Germany and the English Defence Leage (EDL) in Britain. These far-right nationalist groups present themselves as "anti-Islamisation" campaigners. A closer analysis of the lower level foot soldiers reveals them to be 1970s style racists who have found Islamophobia to be a convenient cover for their racism and xenophobia against Asians, Africans and Arabs. Since not much intelligence is found amongst them, these lower-level groups are manipulated, coordinated and given tactical support by others who have their own agendas. For example, Rabbi Nachum Shifren, a right-wing Zionist hardliner from America, visited England in October 2010 to give direction and support to the EDL. In a speech he gave to the EDL, he claimed the group is a salvation of the West from "Muslim dogs".[103] The activities of Tommy Robinson and the EDL are centred around using the crimes committed by sinful Muslims – which are in fact prohibited in Islāmic law and deserve capital punishment – to vilify Islām and stoke anti-Islām hatred among the populations of Western nations.

On the whole, far-right nationalist groups take genuine issues of concern for populations in Europe (such as immigration and crime) and exploit them for their own nefarious agendas. They use them as bait and merchandise to spread their extremist ideology of hate against Islām and Muslims in general. Immigration policies are not being devised and imposed on European nations by Muslims. They are tied to liberal philosophies and adventurous conflicts and wars that Western governments have embarked upon in foreign lands over the past few decades. The governments of countries participating in these wars

---

[103] "Rabbi Shifren's Speech at the EDL Demonstration" reported in the Jewish Chronicle, 25 October 2010.

have agreements between themselves to accommodate refugees created by their military engagements or their active support for revolutions in foreign lands. Thus, whilst patriotically supporting armed forces engaged in overseas conflicts or governments meddling in other countries' politics, right-wing, xenophobic groups should happily welcome the refugees thereby created. If not, then they should make clear their strong opposition to these unneeded interventions and unjust wars whilst they protest against what they see of the adverse effects of immigration upon the economies and identities of European nations, as well as the safety of their inhabitants.

The combined activities of these three groups – between which there are clear alliances and support for each other – help create an atmosphere of distrust, suspicion and animosity against innocent, ordinary Muslims who despise the extremists and terrorists as much as the populations of Western nations despise them, if not even more.

26. How can Muslims combat extremism and terrorism?

Firstly, Muslims must return and adhere to the authentic Prophetic traditions (Sunnah) which comprise perfect guidance in this matter. Extremism occurs when this guidance is abandoned, not followed. The Prophet (peace be upon him) warned severely against extremism and stated in an authentic, well-known tradition: "The extremists are perished, the extremists are perished, the extremists are perished." The Prophetic traditions regarding the Khārijite extremist renegades are known and famous and have been cited earlier. However, widespread ignorance of these realities as well as the poisonous ideology carried by umbrella groups of the Muslim Brotherhood have made generations of Muslims over the past few decades to become affected by this evil, virulent ideology.

The first step is educating oneself, one's family and the society about the roots of this ideology, the ways in which it manifests, its associated religious rhetoric and how and why it clashes with Islām. None have refuted this Khārijite ideology and warned against it so systematically, powerfully and consistently than the Salafī scholars, and their prolific writings can be referred to in this regard. **Secondly**, numerous Salafī scholars – such as Aḥmad al-Najmī, 'Ubayd al-Jābirī – have made clear that Islāmic law permits cooperation with non-Muslim governments in combating crimes which are condemned by Islām such as drug trafficking and terrorism. Muslims are obligated to inform the authorities of any individuals who are involved in planning terrorist attacks or are actively recruiting for terrorist organisations such as ISIS. **Thirdly**, one must not be deceived by their claims of defending and honouring Islām. This is a lie. The Prophet informed his nation that "They will speak with the best, most-alluring speech" whilst describing them as "Dogs of Hellfire" and "The most evil of creation". He encouraged his nation to fight and kill them under the authority of the leaders and reviled them for their outward, apparent acts of devotion which are not genuine but in vain. **Fourthly**, Muslims must not be deceived by extremists who use injustices and calamities befalling Muslims in various lands as cheap merchandise to deceive and draw naive Muslims into their web of extremism. They are skilled in using this method of manipulating the genuine, sincere emotions of Muslims who are deeply hurt by gross injustices against Muslims in places such as Palestine and Burma and the glaring hypocrisy of Western media and governments in how they tend to label terrorism as terrorism only when it is qualified by "Islāmic" but remain silent or inactive about the terrorism committed against Muslims in parts of the world. The extremists thrive upon these issues and use them to convince Muslims of the misguided caliphate-centric ideology of the Khārijite renegades which does not solve any of these problems in reality. **Fifthly**, Muslims must remain devout, upright members of society whose dealings are always based upon justice so that they are true representatives of the dignity and honour that Islām requires from its adherents in all circumstances. The Prophet (peace be upon him) is the best model and guide in all of this.

27. How can Non-Muslims assist Muslims in combating extremism?

Firstly, do not take your knowledge of Islām from Fox News, fundamentalist evangelical Christians, the EDL, extreme right-wing elements, the gutter (tabloid) press and fraudulent pseudo-experts on extremism such as Steven Emerson. There are many groups with political agendas across Europe and America who are actively involved in misinformation and spreading hatred against Muslims and Islām. The deplorable terrorism of ISIS merely provides them a convenient and perfect cover. **Secondly**, realise that Muslims, like most people, are just simply trying to get along with their daily lives and occupations. There are "bad apples" in every group and in Western countries there is a small minority of Muslims involved in criminal activities. They are ignorant people who have been put to trial by the personal desires of wealth, lust and fame and are certainly not motivated by Islām in committing their crimes. In fact, the crimes they commit would be subject to capital punishments if Islāmic law was applied to them. **Thirdly**, keep in mind that common Muslims are under siege from two opposing directions. The first is the promotion of a distorted, extremist, cult ideology – Khārijite Takfīrī-Jihādism – by a very small, outcast, yet vocal minority which is very sadly given far too much media coverage. The second is the promotion of an extremely watered-down version of Islām by governments which demand Muslims to sacrifice their devoutness, modesty, dignity and honour in areas which have no connection to extremism or terrorism at all. This leads to disaffected Muslims who then become easy game for the rhetoric of the extremists. **Fourthly**, if you know any Muslims or come across them, tell them as a well-informed non-Muslim that you know Islām does not condone the terrorism which is perpetrated by al-Qaeda and ISIS. Just as Muslims must also make every effort to convey the same message and openly speak out against the extremists and terrorists at every opportunity. This type of frank dialogue and exchange will help to remove misunderstandings and tensions between communities.

28. Does Islām denigrate women?

Since the 1990s, very large numbers of people in the West have been accepting Islām. Due to increased media coverage of Muslims within the context of global conflicts, more and more people have shown interest in Islām and its teachings. Access to unbiased sources of information about Islām has been made easy through the Internet. The trend in conversions has continued till now and **the majority of converts are women** who outnumber male converts with **a ratio of four to one**.[104] This is despite the extremely negative media coverage

---

[104] As reported in "Women and Conversion to Islām: The American Women's Experience" by Elkoubaiti Naoualv, 2010. News headlines over the past twenty years abound in this regard: "Fast-growing Islām Winning Converts in the Western World", CNN, 14 April 1997. "Why are so Many Modern British

in light of acts of terrorism and claims that Islām denigrates women. The converts are typically well-educated, in professional occupations, come from a variety of backgrounds and include Christians, Jews, Hindūs and Sikhs. This reveals that inquisitive rational, thinking people who are fair-minded and are willing to look beyond the propaganda are finding intellectual and spiritual satisfaction which materialist societies and other religions have been unable to offer them.

It is not our intent to discuss the topic of women's rights in Islām in detail here. We can simply ask the question: What is attracting these women to Islām? Many are disillusioned with Christianity and its confusing theology that a critical mind is unable to decipher. Mystery does not offer satisfactory answers about divinity and many of these women converts state that they find a clear and intelligible treatment of divinity in Islām. Others discover the great honour that Islām confers upon women, contrary to all the propaganda in the media. Others find stability in their lives due to the moral certitude provided by Islāmic teachings compared to hazy, contradictory notions of morals in other philosophies and religions. Many see that women are objectified and exploited in Western societies and come to the realisation that slogans such as "women's rights" and "women's freedom" are shallow, meaningless and hypocritical, especially when sales of goods depend upon naked women and female prostitution is made a taxable occupation. Others have found an antidote in Islām to the mind virus of militant feminism which infects women and causes them to metamorphosise into spiteful monsters far removed from their natural, gentler side. The reasons are many and diverse and cannot all be

---

Career Women Converting to Islām", Daily Mail, 28 October 2010. "Europeans Increasingly Converting to Islam", Gatestone Institute, 27 January 2012. "Converting to Islām: British Women on Prayer, peace and Prejudice", Guardian UK, 11 October 2013. "Rise of Islāmic Converts Challenges France", NY Times, 2 February 2013. "Converts to Islām increase after French attack", World Bulletin, 24 February 2015. "More in France are Turning to Islām, Challenging a Nation's Idea of Itself", NY Times, 3 February 2013. "Islām is Ireland's Fastest Growing Religion", International Business Times, 21 February 2014. This article points out that most of the converts are women. "Lifting the Veil on Ireland's Fastest Growing Religion", Independent Ireland, 21 September 2014. "Islām Growing in America", US Department of Defence, 4 October 2001. "Hispanic Islāmic Converts Find Comfort in God and Latino Culture", Huffington Post, 11 September 2012.

enumerated. Secularists, atheists, militant feminists and many other groups are both grieved and baffled by this phenomenon.

The reason for the tremendous propaganda against women in Islām is because secular, socialist societies exploit women for commercial objectives and to advance collectivist agendas that require the family unit and traditional values to be eroded. The woman is not given any unique, special rights in such societies, but is manipulated through social engineering into roles and behaviours that have little to do with genuine liberation of women but more to do with dismantling the family institution [which provides the basis for inheritance and private property rights] and exploiting women as an under-tapped labour force to expand the reach of taxable economies. In addition, corporate interests see women as huge markets ready to be exploited for profit at the expense of personal interests of women which include health, modesty and chastity. This is aided by promoting liberal philosophies and lifestyles. Many Western women become disillusioned, feel out of touch with their inner selves and yearn for something that will give true meaning, purpose and satisfaction to their lives.

The woman plays a central and crucial role in the family as a mother, sister and daughter. She is a school in herself and plays an instrumental role in building the nation. Given this immense role, she is prone to harassment, discrimination and exploitation in every society without exception. European history bears witness to this indisputable fact right into the early 20th century. Because of this, and because the family unit is of the utmost importance in Islām, the Muslim woman has been given multiple layers of protection through a specific social and economic structure along with a wide range of guaranteed rights that makes it difficult to harass and exploit her. As for that which takes place in Muslim countries of oppression of women and withholding of their rights, then that returns to cultural influences and is far from the lofty ideal that Islām demands with respect to women.

The Prophet (peace be upon him) granted Muslim women the rights of **education**, **possession**, **property**, **inheritance**, **buying**, **selling**, **contracting**, **renting**, **lending**, **mortgaging**, **sponsoring**, **guaranteeing**, **complaining**, **suing**, **freedom of expression** and **keeping her family name** amongst others. Most of these rights were not available to European women until the 19th and 20th centuries. They were only granted with much reluctance on behalf of men, after lengthy campaigns and violence in some cases.

It is true that cultural norms and practices in Muslim lands vary and can and do interfere with women's rights, leading to abuse, but they are not to be confused with Islām. A genuinely God-fearing Muslim will never abuse females. The Prophet (peace be upon him) was of noble, dignified character and strongly emphasised mercy, gentleness and compassion towards women. He said: "The best of you are those who are the best to their women."

29. What is Shiism?

The origins of the Shiite and Khārijite sects are closely intertwined. They were the first two sects to break away from Islām and arose out of the same political circumstances. Both groups excommunicated the companions of the Prophet, developed political ideologies based upon extremist beliefs and fought against the Muslim authorities for political power.

ʿAbdullāh bin Sabaʾ was the individual who played a part in the revolt which eventually led to the assassination of ʿUthmān and the subsequent appearance of the Khārijites and Shiites. The same individual began to exaggerate the status of ʿAlī, the fourth caliph, and claimed he was the rightful heir to political leadership after the Prophet. Then ʿAlī was claimed to have been the intended recipient of the Qurʾān instead of Muḥammad (peace be upon him). Then he was claimed to have been inhabited by the "Spirit of God". Finally, he was deified and claimed to have been God himself. It was also claimed that the Qurʾān has hidden, esoteric meanings known only to ʿAlī and his offspring. It was claimed that true Islām could only be known and conveyed through the lineage of ʿAlī. These unIslāmic doctrines laid the foundations for the development and evolution of Shiite theology and political ideology. A movement developed showing loyalty to ʿAlī and his descendants, seeking revenge for what they claimed to be the usurpation of power from ʿAlī after the Prophet. They excommunicated virtually all of the Prophet's companions and the movement was revolutionary at its core. They became known as the **Shiites** (partisans of ʿAlī) and despite their allegiance to ʿAlī, they caused much consternation and harm to ʿAlī, his family and offspring who are referred to collectively as **Ahl al-Bayt** (People of the Household).

In order to support their novel doctrines, they began to give esoteric explanations to Qurʾānic verses. Throughout the centuries they, just like the Khārijite sect, have been engaged in revolutions against

Muslims in North Africa, the Middle East and Central Asia. Many esoteric movements adopted the face of Shiism as a veil to infiltrate Islām and its people.[105] Today, the main body of Shiites is concentrated in Irān (formerly **Zoroastrian Persia**) which has proxies in the Sunnī lands. It supports and directs these proxies to fulfil the political goals of Shiism which are driven by an underlying desire to see "Persia" gain ascendancy over "Arabia".

Their core beliefs contradict Islām and its monotheistic message. For example, they believe that their leaders have the "Spirit of God"[106] in them and that they have control over life, death, benefit and harm. They believe that pilgrimage can be performed at the graves of their leaders and that they can be invoked and solicited for help and rescue. They also believe that their spiritual leaders have a rank greater than that of the prophets of God and control every atom in the universe. These and many other beliefs are explicitly stated in the books of their leaders such as "The Islāmic Government" (al-Ḥukumāh al-Islāmiyyah) of al-Khomeinī, however, the doctrine of dissimulation (taqiyah) allows them to conceal their beliefs. They believe there is an awaited hidden imām from the offspring of ʿAlī who will appear at the end times when the world will be witnessing revolution and turmoil. They claim that this imām will lead the Shiites to annihilate Sunnī Muslims, take control of Mecca and Medina and restore leadership to its rightful owners. Al-Khomeinī of Irān outlined a doctrine known as the **Guardianship of the Jurist** (wilāyat al-faqīh) in which a supreme leader assumes the role of deputy for the awaited imām and retains divine authority until his arrival. Today, al-Qaeda and ISIS (Khārijites) and Irān (Shiites) along with its proxies in Lebanon, Yemen, Baḥrain, Saudi Arabia and elsewhere are engaged in seditious activities against the ruling authorities and populations of the Gulf countries. There are common

---

[105] The Bāṭiniyyah (esoteric) groups include the Qarāmiṭah, ʿUbaydiyyah, Qāzilbāsh, Khurramiyah, Ḥashshāshīn and others. They brought together a mixture of Persian, Magian beliefs, Greek philosophy and the external face of Shiism as a means of drawing Muslims away from the Prophetic traditions and into esoteric beliefs and practices.

[106] Hence, the title of "Rūḥullāh" (The Spirit of God) that is given to their leaders. It represents the notion that God inhabited ʿAlī and that he continues to inhabit the spiritual leaders of the Shiites who must be obeyed absolutely as possessors of divine authority.

objectives shared between the Shiites and Khārijites, even if they oppose and fight each other at times and places. Al-Qaeda members have admitted receiving tactical support from Irān.[107] Both Khārijism (the ideology of al-Qaeda and ISIS) and Shiism are revolutionary in nature. Their origins lie in the same set of historical circumstances.

30. What is "Wahhabism"?

The word "Wahhabism" is used as a derogatory term to refer to **Muḥammad bin ʿAbd al-Wahhāb** (d. 1792) and his monotheistic reform movement in the Najd region of the Arabian peninsula. Contrary to popular misconception, this area was not under the control of the Ottomans but was ruled by local chiefs who were often engaged in war with each other. Seeing that people across the region had opposed revelation, reason and common sense by worshipping dead saints, trees, stones, idols and other deities, he set out on a program of educational reform but never initiated violence or war. He began to teach the common people to invoke and worship God alone and sent courteous letters to prominent religious and political figures informing them of what he was calling to and clarifying any misconceptions. However, he was met with sectarian antagonism and hostility, leading him to seek protection through an alliance with **Muḥammad bin Saud** (d. 1765) who was the ruler of al-Dirʿiyyah. The Ottoman and Egyptian authorities were incited by rumours and claims that Muḥammad bin ʿAbd al-Wahhāb and his followers had been calling to heresy and disbelief, excommunicating Muslims and killing them. Due to these claims, armed opposition was made against this reform movement. In his numerous refutations of his opponents and detractors, Ibn ʿAbd al-Wahhāb explained that there is nothing which he called to that was outside the canonical four schools of thought in Islām (Ḥanafī, Mālikī, Shāfiʿī, Ḥanbalī). He also stated that he did not make generalised excommunication (takfīr) of the masses, but granted them the excuse of ignorance. He also explained that he only engaged in war as a means of repelling aggression towards his activities of peaceful

[107] Cooperation between Irān and al-Qaeda is now well documented and openly admitted by former al-Qaeda members who cite the existence of "common objectives" behind the material assistance given to them by Irān for a lengthy period stretching ten years or more which included residency, supplies and free passage in and out of Irān.

preaching. He explained that he only fought the stubborn opposers who fought him after they had been convinced that his call was identical to that of the Prophet and not a deviation from it. A product of this historical alliance between the scholar (Ibn ʿAbd al-Wahhāb) and the ruler (Muḥammad bin Saud) is the modern state of Saudi Arabia.

Historical opposition to this reform movement and political opposition towards Saudi Arabia in the modern era comes from numerous orientations. They include the **Khārijite movements** such as al-Ikhwān, al-Qaeda and ISIS, the **Shiites** of Irāq and Irān; the **Ṣūfīs** of the Ottoman era and those across the Muslim world whose religious observances include veneration and worship of saints; **Baʿthists** during the era of Saddām Ḥussain; **Socialists** such as Muʿammār al-Ghaddāfī of Libya and the **Nuṣayrī Alawītes** of Syria.

A great deal of propaganda has been written and spread by these orientations due to religious or sectarian bias that feeds into their wider political agendas. Rarely do Western academics write on the topic of "Wahhābism" without falling prey to much of this propaganda that has accumulated over the past two centuries. Saudi Arabia's Islāmically permissible involvement and contractual agreements with foreign governments in relation to its oil reserves is frequently used by Khārijites as part of their propaganda that Saudi Arabia is behind all the evils taking place in the Muslim world. In a similar way, Western politicians, academics and watch groups pin the source of the extremism and terrorism of ISIS and al-Qaeda to Saudi Arabia or to "Wahhābism." Whilst Saudi Arabia is certainly conservative, it is not the actual source of extremist, terrorist ideology, but the greatest and ultimate target of it through groups such as al-Qaeda and ISIS.

31. What is Salafism?

The word "Salaf" means "predecessor" and "Salafism" refers to an the way of the Prophet and his companions (the predecessors), in their understanding and practice of Islām, free of all later aberrations which led to the appearance of sects and opposing doctrinal schools of thought. It is simply a shorthand way of representing the authentic, pure form of Islām. It is spuriously associated with Jamāl al-Dīn al-Afghānī, an Iranian revolutionary Shiite of the 19th century and also with 20th century Takfīrī-Jihādī ideology. This is due to misinformed writings of Western academics who are either ignorant of elementary Islāmic theology and early Islāmic history or merely pretend to be.[108]

A brief survey of the relevant topics in these areas would immediately inform them that Khārijite Takfīrī-Jihādism is antithetical to Salafism and first emerged in violent opposition to it. Since the Prophet and his companions are the "Salaf" (emulated model), it is impossible to qualify groups like al-Qaeda and ISIS as "Salafist" because their ideological ancestors, the Khārijites, waged war against the "Salaf" as has preceded. The very first Takfīrī-Jihādists assassinated the third and fourth caliphs ʿUthmān and ʿAlī, attempted to assassinate the Prophet's companions who ruled over Syria and Egypt and continued to revolt against the first ruling dynasty, the Umayyads. The foundation of their revolt was the accusation that those rulers were unjust, did not judge by God's law and had become apostates.

In the writings and books of the "Salafist" scholars starting with **ʿUmar bin ʿAbd al-ʿAzīz** (d. 720) and **Wahb bin Munabbih** (d. 728), there can be found a consistent, strong and robust rebuttal of this group and its core principles over a period of 1300 years till this day of ours. This stern position towards the Khārijite Takfīrī Jihādists has been inherited by the followers of Salafism in every generation and their writings in those 1300 years are an ample testimony to this fact.

---

[108] In the time of the Prophet, due to the absence of deviation from his guidance, there was only one name for pure Islām: **Islām**. When the Khārijite and Shiite extremists appeared, the Prophet's companions began to call to adherence to the Sunnah (Prophetic traditions) and the united main body under the authority of the ruler (Jamāʿah). Thus, a distinction was made between Muslims following right guidance who were known as **Ahl al-Sunnah wal-Jamāʿah** (The People of Prophetic Traditions and Unity) and Muslims who entered the deviant sects. When further heresies led to the emergence of other sects, such as the Qadarites, Murjites and the Jahmites who introduced speculative theology based upon philosophy, the students of the Prophet's companions and their students began to make reference to the necessity of following the way of **al-Salaf al-Ṣāliḥ**. (The Righteous Predecessors). There are many documented statements in this regard and the usage of the appellation of "Salafī" is known and documented from the 2nd century hijrah which is around the late 8th century CE. In all subsequent works of Muslim scholars expounding the correct Islāmic belief and methodology, repeated reference is made to the "Salaf", meaning the Prophet, his companions and their students. Hence, the claim that "Salafism" is a modern movement is spurious and baseless.

The Salafī scholar and former Muftī of Saudi Arabia, **ʿAbd al-ʿAzīz bin Bāz** (d. 1999) declared the Takfīrī-Jihādist Khārijites as disbelievers who are not even in the fold of Islām. Deviant sects in Islām are known through the erroneous principle(s) that uniquely identify them. Even if they were in total agreement in every other matter, if they erred in just one foundational principle, they would not escape the judgement of having become a deviated sect. This is precisely the nature of the very first sects that appeared such as the Khārijites, Shiites, Qadarites, Murjites and others throughout Islāmic history. Just because a group assumes the label of "Salafist", the mere claim does not make them so until and unless all of their principles are in complete agreement with the way of the Salaf. In this regard, all 20th century Takfīrī-Jihādist movements are no different from the very first Khārijites who claimed they were better guided than the Prophet's companions, despite the fact that they never took knowledge from the Prophet, nor from his companions. Their claim to orthodoxy was spurious. Similarly, the Khārijite Takfīrī Jihādists of the 21st century who claim to be "Salafist", their claim to "Salafism" is also spurious because they never studied with the contemporary Salafī scholars. They are known to these scholars only as **extremists** and **terrorists** who combined the doctrines of their Khārijite ancestors with European revolutionary ideology.

Despite these theological and historical facts well known to Salafi scholars for 1300 years, the fabricated and academically dishonest label of "Salafī-Jihādist" has been used to describe these terrorists. It is alleged that "Salafists" are of three groups: The **Quietists** who adhere to peaceful preaching, the **Activists** who engage in politics to assert influence and the **Jihādists** who use violence and terrorism. This is a fallacious categorisation which has found its way into academia, government bodies and intelligence agencies all of whom are victims of Khārijite propaganda which they have taken at face value. A working knowledge of elementary Islāmic theology would inform the scrupulous academic that it is impossible for the second two groups to be "Salafist" due to their violation of one of the greatest principles of Islām as enunciated so clearly in the Qurʾān, the Prophetic traditions, the statements of the Prophet's companions and the statements and writings of all the famous scholars of the Muslims. These scholars include ʿAbdullāh bin al-Mubārak (d. 797), Aḥmad bin Ḥanbal (d. 855), Ibn Taymiyyah (d. 1328), and Muḥammad Ibn ʿAbd al-Wahhāb (d.

1792) who have well known, oft-quoted statements in this regard. This principle is: Anyone who contends with the ruler of the Muslims for power whether physically or by encouraging it verbally – even if he himself does not engage in violence and revolt – upon the ideological conviction that the sinful, tyrannical ruler has left Islām and does not deserve obedience is from the heretical Khārijtes. Claiming to be "Salafist" does not avail such a person in anything. This was the first deviation in Islām and is totally antithetical to Salafism. This principle is mentioned as the consensus of the Muslims in the books of early Salafī scholars such as "The Foundations of the Sunnah" by Imām Aḥmad bin Ḥanbal (d. 855) and is found repeated throughout the centuries till we reach the era of the contemporary Salafī scholars.

The Khārijites can never be Salafist by definition, it is a theological and historical impossibility. They may be accurately referred to as **Takfīrī-Jihādist Khārijites** as we have established in this work. Their roots lie in challenging the integrity and authority of the Prophet (peace be upon him) and killing the Prophet's closest companions. They assassinated two righteous caliphs of Islām, ʿUthmān and ʿAlī, and attempted to assassinate the deputy rulers of Egypt and Syria, both of whom were companions of the Prophet.

Qualifying them as "Salafī-Jihādists" or "Quietist-Jihādists" is an enormous error and when done with knowledge and intent is a sign of ignorance, historical revisionism, or academic dishonesty.

The very first "Salaf" (righteous predecessor) for the Muslims is the **Prophet Muḥammad** (peace be upon him), and he said of the "Takfīrī-Jihādist" Khārijites: "They will never cease to appear until the last of them come out alongside the Anti-Christ (Dajjāl), so wherever you meet them, kill them, for they are the most evil of creation."[109] And the late Salafī scholar Muḥammad bin Ṣāliḥ al-ʿUthaymīn (d. 2001) said: "If you were to look into the hearts [of the Khārijite terrorist extremists], you would find them black and hard. They accuse sinful Muslims of disbelief, but they are greater in disbelief."[110] The Khārijites are the greatest enemies of the Salafīs, past and present and will remain so as explicitly stated in these unequivocal, emphatic Prophetic traditions. They appeared making war againt Islām, against its most noble carriers, and they will remain as such till the end of time.

---

[109] Reported by al-Ḥākim in al-Mustadrak (2/147).

[110] Liqāʾ al-Bāb al-Maftūḥ (no. 11).

Concluding notes

Groups like al-Qaeda and ISIS are a product of modern revolutionary ideology mixed with the doctrine of the Khārijite sect that was severely condemned by the Prophet Muḥammad (peace be upon him). Their acts of terrorism are the first enemy to Islām and they are engaged in war against Islām and its people before anyone else. Their existence is of no benefit to Muslims and they are a source of tribulation and calamities. The late Salafī scholar, **Muḥammad bin Ṣāliḥ al-ʿUthaymīn** (d. 2001) said, "When the affair of the Muslim Brotherhood appeared, those who proceed without wisdom, the Westeners' perception of Islām became increasingly disfigured. I am referring to those who throw bombs into crowds of people with the claim that this is jihād in the path of God! The reality is that they have harmed Islām and the people of Islām. A person has to almost cover his face so that he is not associated with this seditious terrorizing faction. Islām is free and innocent of them."[111] These terrorists do not serve the interests of Muslims and are often used and manipulated to facilitate external interests and agendas. The Islāmic ruling upon them is unequivocal and clear: They are extremist renegades, disbelievers (in the view of numerous Muslim scholars) and are to be fought and killed wherever they are found under the leadership of the relevant authorities. Linking them to even conservative forms of Islām such as "Wahhābism" or Salafism, let alone Islām itself, is erroneous in the view of well-informed Western academics. Muslims have contractual obligations in non-Muslim lands which must be honoured. Observant Muslims face many challenges to their faith as they try to live righteous, devout lives and their desire to protect their faith has nothing to do with extremist or terrorist ideology. The very small number of sinful Muslims in Western societies who engage in crimes that Islām condems or the vocal extremists who follow a political ideology that is antithetical to Islām do not represent Islām or the majority of Muslims. Attempts to force a concocted, watered-down version of Islām upon the majority due to the activities of an ignorant, extremist minority are counter-productive and only serve to push more and more people towards the extremists who make reference to these very attempts when trying to recruit disaffected Muslims into their ideology.

---

[111] Refer to Fatāwā ʿUlamā al-Kibār (p. 321-322).

Further Reading

The following are further resources the reader can benefit from with respect to this topic:

Publications

Terrorism and its Effects Upon the Individual and Society
– Shaykh Zayd al-Madkhalī
With Which Intellect and Religiosity is Bombing and Destruction Considered Jihād?
– Shaykh ʿAbd al-Muḥsin al-ʿAbbād
The Rise of Jihadist Extremism in the West
– Salafi Publications
The Noble Revered Prophet of Islām
– Abū Iyaaḍ, Hikmah Publications

Websites

http://www.islamagainstextremism.com
http://www.takfiris.com
http://www.prophetmuhammad.name

Research On Islamophobic Hate Networks

A number of in depth academic research papers expose the funders of hate who help shape public opinion against Muslims:

The Cold War on British Muslims. An examination of Policy Exchange and the Centre for Social Cohesion. For more details and the report, refer to http://www.spinwatch.org.

Fear Inc. The Roots of the Islamophobia Network in America. This in-depth investigation conducted by the Center for American Progress Action Fund reveals not a vast right-wing conspiracy behind the rise of Islamophobia in our nation but rather a small, tightly networked group of misinformation experts guiding an effort that reaches millions of Americans through effective advocates, media partners, and grassroots organising. This spreading of hate and misinformation primarily starts with five key people and their organisations, which are sustained by funding from a clutch of key foundations. Refer to http://www.americanprogress.org.

Appendix: On Atheism

At the simplest level, the atheist position can be illustrated by the following analysis: The knowledge of each individual that he was non-existent and did not create himself or create the means through which he came to be (reproduction) or create the universe is a self-evident truth. Every person knows he did not bring his own self into being from non-being. Likewise, the knowledge that the universe did not create itself and the knowledge that multiple universes do not come into existence except with a cause or force external to the sum of them is a self-evident truth. All of this knowledge is innate, intuitive, necessary and self-evident and is alluded to in the Qur'ān: "**Were they created by nothing? Or are they the creators? Or did they create the Heavens and Earth? Indeed, they have no certainty**." (52:35-36).

Hence, there are only three possibilities. Either "nothing created something else" or "something created itself" which are two ways of saying the same thing, or "something created something else." When each of these three possibilities are presented, all people of sound mind – including unbiased, truthful atheists – will say the latter, that "something created something else" appeals most to common sense and reason and is the soundest of the three propositions. This is intuitive, rational and in accordance with the knowledge gained from the sum of human creative enterprise in all of history. The real debate therefore, is all about the question: **What is this "something" to which creation is attributed?**

It is here that the reality of the difference between a believer in God and an atheist becomes apparent. The atheist, suffering from cosmic authority syndrome and having already decided that only a material explanation for life is acceptable, has simply taken the qualities necessary for creating, conferred them upon "nature" and then reframed these qualities with a play on words. Thus "natural law" is what creates, but it does so "without purpose and direction." He has ascribed such actions to "nature" – matter and its properties – that can only be ascribed to a knowing, willing, powerful, purposeful agent. This sleight of hand is similar to the behaviour of the child who breaks a glass and says it broke itself randomly for no reason, thereby denying causation. He ascribes the performance of an act to the object which is known to all people of sound mind and common sense to have been the recipient of the act, not its performer. "Nature" does not have any inherent, independent, creative ability in and of itself. Rather, "nature" is itself an intricate, complex, interwoven, interdependent nexus of cause-effect mechanisms which have been specifically designed to work the way they do.

One should not be under any illusion that an atheist believes in a "creator" of some sorts because the atheist must have a creation story to account for existence and life. This creation story is that matter self-creates and self-organises through random, non-directed, purposeless events to produce dust, water, DNA, cells, plants, trees, animals, Senator Al Gore and the Internet. This story is built upon a logical impossibility, (self-creation), requires a violation of the universal law of causality (every effect must have an adequate antecedent cause) and contradicts the law of entropy (order always moves to disorder, things always degrade). It is a religious doctrine which asserts a long series of **amazing coincidences** following a hypothetical, conjectural, miraculous "big-bang" expansion. The hard-wired default which atheists attempt to escape from by providing this alternative creation story is belief in a supreme, eternal, all-knowing and all-powerful creator who skilfully creates through his knowledge, will, power and command, not without purpose but for far-reaching wisdoms. He is known through his handiwork which is direct proof of his existence, his attributes and qualities. The very apparent nature of the universe and biological life – as studied and described in tens of millions of scientific research papers through the inescapable use of language that must assume design, purpose and contrivance – is powerful evidence for the existence of a creator. Knowing this is a compelling argument, atheists like Richard Dawkins demand that people must distrust their own physical senses. They require people to discard self-evident truths and believe that all the wonders of the universe and life they observe around them are merely "illusions" of design and not actual design, produced by "mountains of probability", "blind watchmakers", "selfish-genes" and hundreds of "amazing coincidences." Distrust of the physical senses and rejection of what is very apparent to sensory perception is a sign of delusion and madness.[112]

This creation story requires a much larger leap of faith and is the reason why in the whole of history, the overwhelming majority of humanity has never strayed from its innate, natural default of belief in a supreme

---

[112] Tony Rothman, American theoretical physicist, wrote: "When confronted with the order and beauty of the universe and the strange coincidences of nature, it's very tempting to take the leap of faith from science into religion. I am sure many physicists want to. I only wish they would admit it." Refer to "Paradigms Lost" by John Casti, (Avon Books, 1989) p.482-483. Despite the presence of these types of admissions, prior conviction and commitment to materialism forces atheists to attribute design to "nature" (a combination of matter, its properties and the laws of physics) which is a veiled way of saying that matter is able to self-organise in a seemingly intelligent way by pure chance (random undirected processes).

creator.[113] No matter how one looks at it, every single person, atheist or otherwise, must have one entity which is eternal as part of their creation story. And that entity must possess qualities and perform actions that lead to what we observe around us in all its wondrous complexity. The innate, natural default is that this eternal "something" that did the creating is God, the Lord of the worlds, the all-knowing, all-powerful, all-wise, masterful creator. This would mean that there is intrinsic direction, purpose and meaning to every person's life. To the atheist materialist however, this eternal "something" is matter. It randomly self-organises without purpose in a process that can create life. This means there is no ultimate direction, true purpose or meaning to life, it just comes and goes in pure randomness, and every person must invent and pursue his own purpose in life. Nothing but conjecture supports this creation story and it is demanded by a previously held philosophical conviction in materialism. "**And they say: 'There is nothing but our life of this world, we die and we live and nothing destroys us except the passing of time.' Of this, they have no knowledge, they merely conjecture**." (Qur'ān 45:24).

The true and real difference then, once all the layers are peeled and we get to the crux of the matter, is whether "creation" – and of the type and complexity that is observed – comes from a knowing, willing, powerful, purposeful being or from disorderly, coincidental randomness. The first position is an affirmation of reason and the foundation of all scientific inquiry which must assume that the universe and life are rationally

---

[113] There are **three levels** in the atheist pyramid. **The first level**, at the very top, and the minority, are those who readily acknowledge that "naturalism" or "materialism" is simply a preferred world-view and that there is nothing in the institution of science that compels such a world view. This includes scientists such as Richard Lewontin (evolutionary biologist) and Thomas Nagel (atheist philosopher). **The second level** consists of the aggressive "new atheists" such as Richard Dawkins who assert a level of certainty and conviction for their naturalist, materialist dogma on the basis of conjectures that the scientific method does not validate. They misrepresent the current state of scientific knowledge and present their conjectures and assertions as indisputed facts. **The third** are the majority, and they are the common riff-raff at the bottom who are dominated and governed intellectually by the second level above them. They are oblivious to the atheists at the top who make frank admissions that naturalism or materialism is assumed preferentially not scientifically and that the institution and instruments of science cannot positively assert such a world-view as it is outside the capabilities of the domain of science. This does call into question the integrity of the second level of atheists who pretend to be driven by science but are in fact motivated by psychological and emotional reasons.

intelligible and this can only be if they are designed to be that way. The second position is a revilement of reason and is based upon a prior conviction in and commitment to materialist philosophy.[114]

Thus, the issue comes down to **choosing** between whether that which appears designed and purposeful comes about through self-creation and random, undirected processes (chance) or through knowledge, will, power and wisdom. The **true empirical scientific method** will always prove the latter and will never, ever prove the former, which is but mere conjecture. It is built upon **prior conviction** in materialist philosophy and propped up by theoretical physics in which what is imaginary and exists in the mind only is made actual and real through clever mathematics, not empirical science.

---

[114] It is vital to distinguish between two different definitions of science. **The first definition** of science is "observation, theorization, experimentation, collection of data, and making inferences and explanations with impartiality". This is a standard definition of science and the process it represents is one from which, in a modern-context, we gain an understanding of the material world that allows us to produce cars, washing machines, airplanes, medicine and so on and it includes investigating causes and effects and the special properties of things. This "scientific method" has been applied and harnessed to allow the beneficial interests of humankind to be realized and safeguarded through a gradual understanding of the system of interconnected causes and effects which are referred to as "nature" by materialists and "creation" by believers in God. This first definition of science presupposes and affirms order, regularity and rationality in the universe. The natural disposition of humans is imprinted with this affirmation. Thus, non-conjectural, empirical science can never conflict with belief in God, keeping in mind that the human capacity to fully understand the reality of "nature" is severely limited. **The second definition** is "the explanation of all phenomena through natural, materialistic causes only". This is really a philosophical assertion, that only natural causes exist. Providing material explanations (of causes and effects) in the study of the world is not really an issue and does not clash with the Islāmic understanding of how the universe or life operate, since affirmation of the ways and means and causes and effects and of the inherent properties in things that collectively comprise the "natural causes" is established in the Qur'ān and Prophetic traditions. However, the real intent behind this second definition of science is to credit nature (physical law and random events acting upon matter) with an illusion of design that we allegedly observe when we explore and study life and the universe, and then to consider this to be the only "rational foundation" that must underpin all scientific enquiry and its conclusions. From here arises Richard Dawkins' "blind-watchmaker", "mountain of improbability" and the "nothing" of Lawrence Krauss and Stephen Hawking from which "the universe can and will create itself". It is here that we move away from empirical science based upon actual physical reality and instead to the land of fairy tales where that which exists only in the mind is made to appear real and actual through creative mathematical witchcraft.